Do-It-Yourself

Includes online audio & instructional video

VIOLIN

BY HENRIETTE DE VRIJER

PLAYBACK+
Speed • Pitch • Balance • Loop

To access audio and video, visit:
www.halleonard.com/mylibrary

Enter Code
5996-6812-9442-9415

I0802804

Violin Recordings by Niki Yerakaris

ISBN 978-1-70515-109-9

HAL•LEONARD®

Visit Hal Leonard Online at
www.halleonard.com

World headquarters, contact:
Hal Leonard
7777 West Bluemound Road
Milwaukee, WI 53213
Email: info@halleonard.com

In Europe, contact:
Hal Leonard Europe Limited
1 Red Place
London, W1K 6PL
Email: info@halleonardeurope.com

In Australia, contact:
Hal Leonard Australia Pty. Ltd.
4 Lentara Court
Cheltenham, Victoria, 3192 Australia
Email: info@halleonard.com.au

FOREWORD

Welcome to *Do-It-Yourself Violin*.

In this book, you will be taken on a journey of learning to play the violin. Whether you are a complete beginner, a re-starter, or just playing the pieces in this book for fun, I hope that you will enjoy developing your violin playing.

This book will take you step-by-step through the different stages of learning to play. You will begin by learning how to hold the instrument and the bow, and how to take your first bow strokes. You will also learn how to read music and play familiar songs.

By the end of this book, you will have reached an intermediate playing level on your violin and have the skills to be able to explore new pieces by yourself.

I am Henriette, your guide, and I am delighted to take you on this adventure. I am an experienced violin teacher. My pupils, who range in age from 5 to 85, come from all walks of life and are located all over the world. Despite their diversity, all my students have one thing in common: they love to play pieces they know. By learning how to play the violin with this book, you will become a part of this community of players too. I hope that you will have lots of fun in the meantime!

INTRODUCTION

This book has 22 chapters, and each chapter is divided into different sections:

1. Violin skills: holding the violin and bow, and exercises to develop your violin playing.
2. Note reading: learning to read music.
3. Playing along: step-by-step guides to learning new pieces and violin techniques.
4. Playing together: playing your newly-learned music with a backing track.

Along the way, you will also find "Toolboxes" and "Violin Talks" that outline the essentials of music theory and violin technique to help you progress faster.

Learning to play the violin—like any new skill—requires regular practice and an openness to explore what happens when you start to learn to play. Besides the milestones that you will achieve, there may also be moments in this journey when you feel challenged. That's okay. Most players do. If you find that Do-It-Yourself learning becomes a lonely business, please don't despair! Help is available in different forms:

Firstly, at the end of this book, there is a troubleshooting section where you may find answers to commonly-asked questions. Secondly, on my YouTube channel: ***www.youtube.com/c/ProAmStrings***, you can find additional videos on playing techniques, how to organize your practice, and so on. Finally, lessons are available, and players sometimes come to me with one particular issue that can be solved in just one lesson, after which DIY learning can continue more smoothly again.

Wishing you many hours of pleasure learning to play the pieces in this book and good luck on your journey of discovery!

Henriette
www.proamstrings.com

About the Video and Audio

Accompanying this book are video and audio tracks. The videos (indicated by the video icon) provide detailed insights about techniques and help you practice your pieces, just like your teacher would help you in a face-to-face lesson. The audio tracks () will allow you to hear how the music sounds and, in some cases, play along with a backing track.

Use the code found on page 1 to access the accompanying video and audio at ***www.halleonard.com/mylibrary***.

Milestones

When you see this icon, you have achieved a milestone in your progress. Time to celebrate your achievement! If you have found things tricky up to this point, go over the previous section again until you have mastered the skills before you carry on. There are seven milestones for you to achieve in total.

LESSON 1:
Getting Started

The Instrument

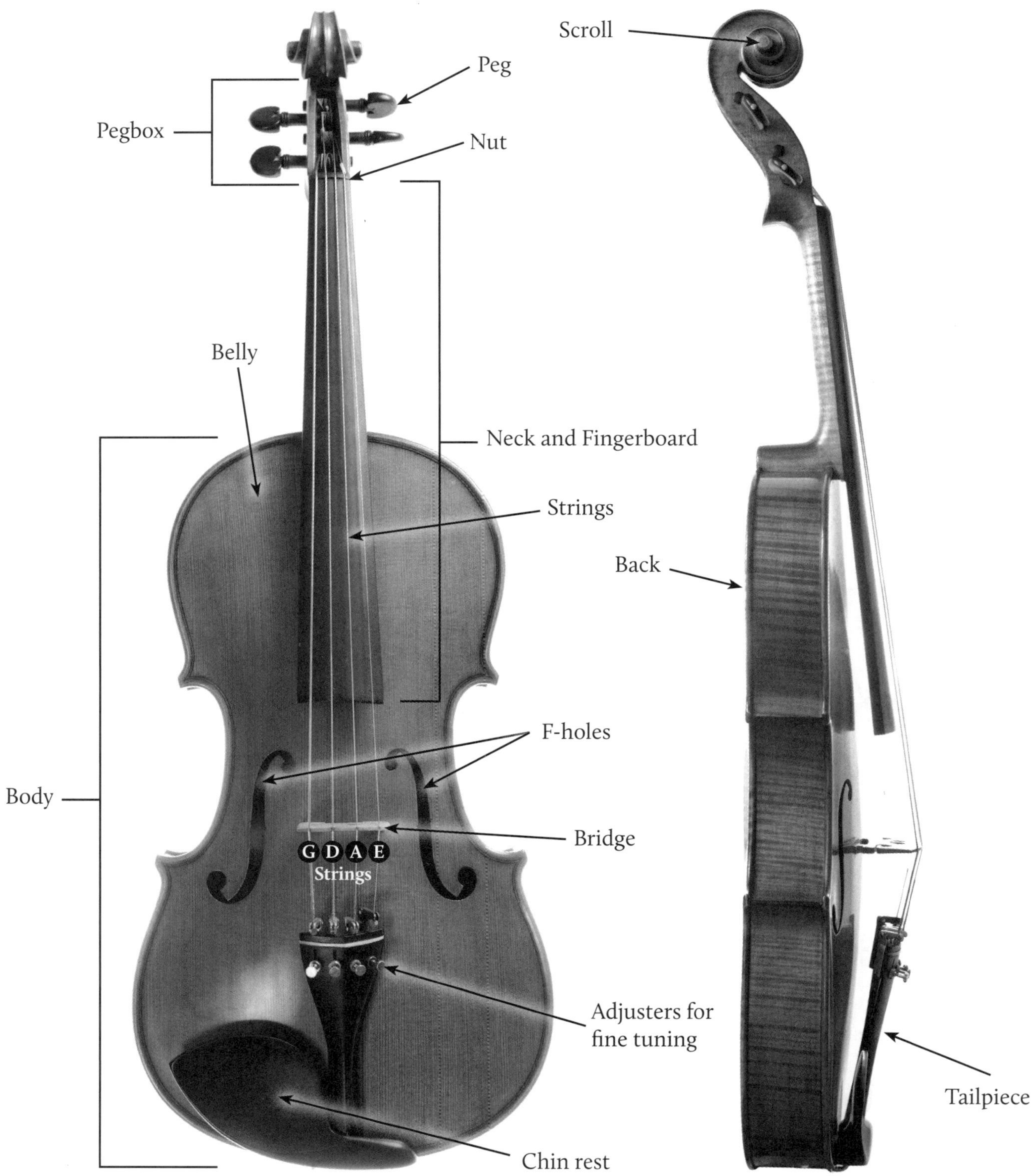

Violins come in different sizes. Children and young people whose fingers are not yet big enough to reach the positions on a full-size violin play on smaller instruments—1/64, 1/32, 1/16, 1/10, 1/8, 1/4, 1/2, 3/4, and 7/8—which get changed over to bigger sizes as they grow. When children are about 12 years old, they move to a full-sized instrument. Adults play on full-sized instruments, unless they are very petite, in which case they may play on a 7/8 sized violin.

A decent quality instrument is vital for progress on the violin. Resist buying an instrument simply because it is cheap. Better quality instruments are made from more responsive wood and therefore sound better. Moreover, better instruments are lighter to hold, built in a more slimline way, and therefore are easier to play. Watch the video for tips on buying an instrument, what makes a suitable instrument, and what to steer clear of.

Is My Instrument Suitable for Learning On?

You may already have an instrument; in that case, you may want to check that it is suitable to learn to play on. We don't want to make learning to play unnecessarily difficult, so it is important that the instrument is properly set up. The instrument set-up is the way the bridge is placed on the belly of the violin. The bridge is a vital part of the violin because it not only determines the height of the strings, but also sets the angle of the strings in relation to each other, and the width between each of the strings. Let's check the set-up of your violin before we start to play.

First, let's check the height of the strings. The height of the strings is determined by the height of the bridge. At the end of the fingerboard where the f-holes are, the strings should be about half a thumbnail above the fingerboard. At the nut—the narrow end of the fingerboard—the strings should vibrate just free from the fingerboard and sit no higher than 2mm above the fingerboard. If you find that the strings on your violin are set higher, you will need to take the instrument to a luthier's workshop to have the strings lowered. This will not be very complicated or costly, but it will be vital for success on the violin.

Second, let's check the angle of the strings on the bridge. Look at the bridge from the tailpiece end. The D-string, second from the left, should be the highest string, and the E-string, furthest to the right, the lowest. Is there a smooth curve?

Lastly, let's check the way the strings are set into the bridge. The strings should be 7 to 8mm apart and evenly spaced. The strings should just be set into the bridge and not so deep that the strings are below the level of the top of the bridge.

Checking that the set-up is right will help make learning to play easier and prevent frustration later.

Strings

Different types of violin strings make very different sounds, from a more direct and full sound, to sounds that are more mellow in character. Advanced players use different types of strings to bring out certain character traits in their instrument. Beginners should choose strings that respond easily to the bow and produce a good quality sound, without having to make much effort with the bow. Therefore, it is important to choose medium price range, long-lasting strings that are easy to tune (e.g. Thomastik Dominant Strings). Don't be tempted to buy the cheapest string you can find online; ask for advice from a local violin shop or dealer. You will have a lot more pleasure from your playing if your violin is sounding at its best!

It is almost inevitable that at some point you accidentally break a string. This occasionally happens during tuning (see *Tuning the Violin,* p. 9), but it may also happen because of temperature changes or through normal wear and tear.

Strings will need replacing from time to time. Depending on how much you play, after a year or two, strings will get old and become less responsive or may not stay in tune. If you have not played your instrument for some time, it is best to have new strings fitted.

When a new string is fitted on the violin, the string will stretch, and it is normal to need to tune that string more frequently until it is fully played in. Initially, your new string may also sound a bit harsh. Again, that will mellow over time. We tend to replace strings one by one and not all four strings at the same time because of the extra tuning and more coarse sound.

Strings, like violins, are natural products, which respond to changes in atmospheric pressure. Therefore, violin players tune their strings each time before playing. Violins should not be left in cars or near a radiator in your home. If a place is too hot or cold for you, it will also be too hot or cold for your instrument.

Some string types are made from a nylon core, wound with silver wire. People with a high amount of hand perspiration may find that the winding of this type of string may come away and you are left with a string that is very uneven and unpleasant to play. If this happens, you may choose to use metal strings, which are more resistant to this kind of wear and tear.

The Bow

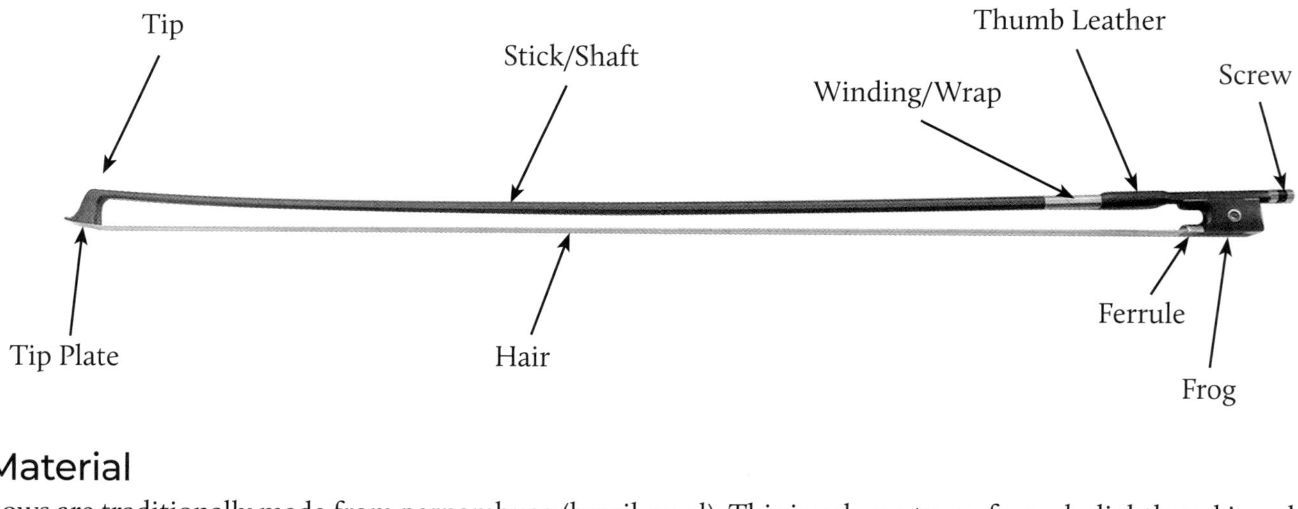

Material

Bows are traditionally made from pernambuco (brazilwood). This is a dense type of wood, slightly red in color and quite flexible, which makes it extremely suitable for bows used in string playing. However, pernambuco is a protected species and therefore expensive, so carbon fiber bows are often used instead. Carbon fiber bows have the added advantage of being slightly stronger, which makes these bows more suitable for beginners.

How Does the Bow Work?

The bow works by "pulling" the string, which makes it vibrate and produce sound. The sound will travel via the bridge into the instrument, which will in turn start to vibrate the column of air inside the violin. This will make the belly and back of the violin vibrate too, which will create the distinctive sound of each instrument. While it is the violin that gives the sound its character, it is the bow that makes the violin sing.

Before playing, the bow hair will need to be tightened. There is a screw at the heel of the bow for tightening. The bow needs to be tight enough so that the stick does not touch the string while playing but not so tight that the bow becomes convex. About a finger width between the hair and the stick will be about right. The bow hair is naturally stretchy and will need to be loosened after each playing. This will allow it to keep its springiness. Looking after your bow, having it re-haired every year, and using rosin on it frequently will give you years of pleasure playing your violin.

Correct Tightness

Too Loose

Too Tight

Accessories

Rosin

Before being able to "pull" the string, you need to apply rosin to the bow. Rosin makes the bow sticky and creates friction when drawing the string. If you don't have any rosin or too little rosin, the bow will slip across the strings and not make any sound.

Rosin is made from the resin of pine trees, which has been prepared and shaped in a rosin factory. Rosin comes in different qualities from softer to harder, which produce different sounds and respond differently in warmer or cooler climates. Generally, the darker-colored rosins are harder and more suitable for hot climates, and the lighter-colored rosins are softer and respond better in cool climates. Much depends on personal preference though, and for a beginner, the price may be a determining factor. For those players who are allergic to some rosin types, there is a hypo-allergenic rosin on the market.

When applying rosin to your bow, first tighten the bow and make sure to cover the metal part of the heel of the bow with your thumb to prevent chipping bits off the rosin. Rub the rosin firmly over the hair in short strokes until it becomes a white powder that sticks to the hair. The rosin should cover the entire length of the bow. Pay particular attention to either end of the bow. A brand-new bow will need quite a lot of rosin to fill up the entire depth of bow hair. Later, you may rosin slightly less.

If there is a layer of dust on the violin after playing, you have too much rosin. If the bow slips across the strings, there may be too little rosin. Rosin the bow each time you play and remove the excess rosin with a soft cloth from the stick and instrument after playing.

Shoulder Rest

To make the violin sit correctly and comfortably on your shoulder, you will need a shoulder rest under the violin. The main purpose of the shoulder rest is to fill the gap between the jaw and collarbone. As each person is different, shoulder rests come in a variety of shapes and sizes. For beginners, a shoulder rest that is flexible and can be shaped to fit the curve of your shoulder is the most suitable. A good shoulder rest is expensive, but will last for years, and will make your playing considerably more comfortable. Perhaps most importantly, learning to play the violin with a well-fitting shoulder rest will help you progress faster than if you learned to play without a shoulder rest. Watch the video in Lesson 2, *Holding the Violin*, to learn how to attach the shoulder rest correctly to your violin and how to shape it to fit your shoulder perfectly.

Music Stand

Many violin players play standing up rather than sitting down because it promotes a good violin hold and playing posture. It is important that your music is at eye height when you play. A music stand at the correct height will help you to have good posture and an easier time playing for longer periods.

Tuning the Violin

Violin strings are tuned G, D, A, and E from the lowest string to the highest (left to right). You will need to tune your violin every time you begin your practice. The pegs are used for roughly getting your strings in tune, and if you have fine tuners, you can use these for getting your strings more precisely in tune. Many players find tuning challenging in the early stages of playing, so don't despair if you are one of them. Good tuning will become easier over time, as you gain experience.

1. Start by tuning the A-string (second from the right). Most players will use an electronic tuner, tuning app, or tuning fork to find the correct pitch of the A-string.
2. If the A-string is significantly out of tune, use the pegs to get close to the correct pitch (it doesn't have to be perfect). Turning the peg away from you will raise the pitch. Turning the peg towards you will lower the pitch.

VIOLIN TALK

When using the pegs for tuning, always loosen the pegs first before tightening them, as you can easily break a string when tightening the pegs too hastily.

3. Use the fine tuners to get your A-string precisely in tune. Turning clockwise will raise the pitch. Turning counterclockwise will lower the pitch.
4. Once the A-string is in tune, sing down the scale to find the pitch of the D-string and repeat steps 2 and 3. Apply the same method for the G-string, followed by the E-string. While you learn to hear these pitches, you can also use a tuning app to find the tunings of the strings.

Violin Maintenance

If you look after your instrument before and after playing, your violin will need very little maintenance. It is a good idea to have your instrument checked over by a luthier about once a year so the instrument can be cleaned, and the bridge adjusted if necessary. Apart from that, all you need to do is dust the rosin off the violin after playing and store the violin in its case whenever it is not being played. The bow hair will need to be tightened before playing and loosened after playing so that the hair will keep its natural stretchiness. You may also dust the rosin off the stick after playing.

LESSON 2:
The First Bow Strokes

This chapter will teach you how to hold the bow and violin and manage your first bow strokes. This is an important part of your violin playing journey because our aim is to set up good habits from the start. Watch and play along with the videos, paying particular attention to the correct movements. At this stage, there is a lot to remember. It doesn't matter if you are not able to manage everything in one go. Revisit the videos frequently in the early days and have another go. You will soon find that you can get more than one aspect of violin playing right at the same time.

Holding the Bow

While a good bow hold has certain features that are required for effective bow control, there is room for individual variation. Each hand is shaped slightly different, and will have small variations in how the bow is balanced.

To make a good bow hold:

1. Create a ring shape with your thumb and middle finger, connecting at the knuckle. Open to create a small gap for the bow to go between. Your thumb and middle finger should always be opposite each other.
2. Place your thumb in the space between the wood of the frog and the protector sleeve on the stick. It will be tempting to place your thumb in the crook of the frog; however, that is incorrect placement.

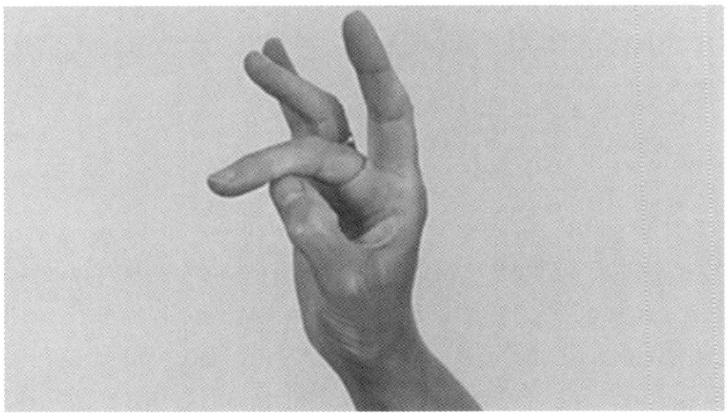

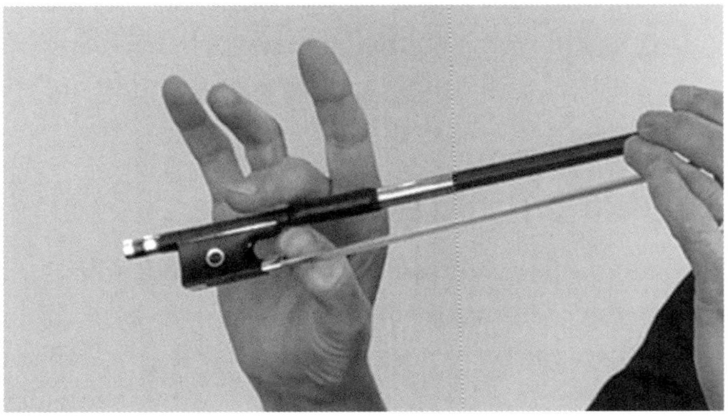

3. Place your index finger a finger-width apart from your middle finger.
4. Place your ring finger next to your middle finger.
5. Place your pinky a finger-width away but on the side edge of the bow, not in line with your other fingers.

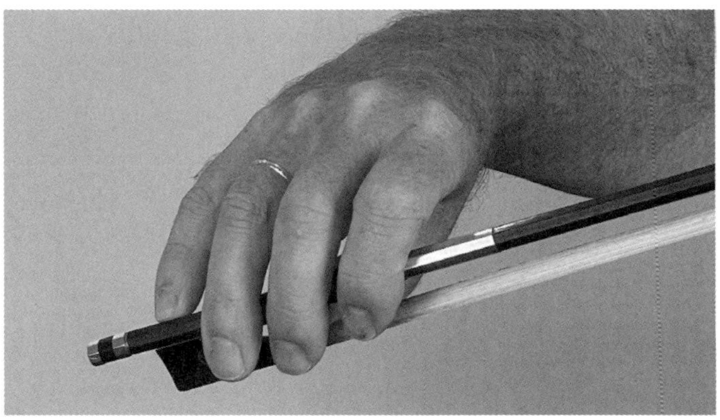

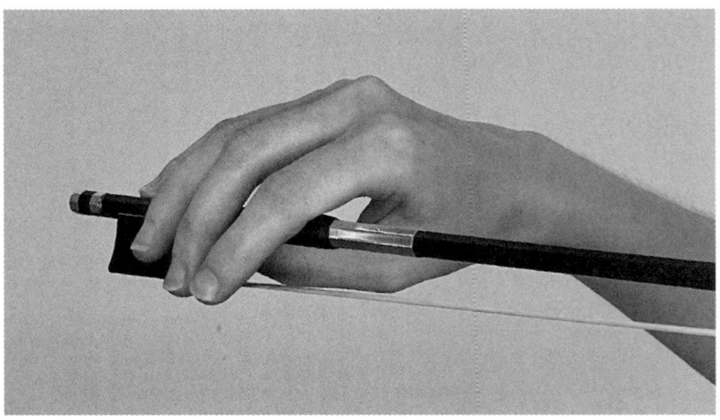

In the early stages of playing, you may find the bow hold quite tight, and this is completely normal. When you become more advanced, you will be able to hold the bow in a more relaxed way, which may change the way your hand is shaped around the bow. A good bow hold is never a finished product and will change in the years to come. That is a good thing. As you progress with your playing, you will develop a more sophisticated bow hold.

Bow Hand Flexibility Exercises

Practice the following exercises to help make the muscles in your bow hand stronger and more flexible. Start and finish each exercise with a proper bow hold.

1. Hold the bow horizontally and wave the bow up and down, flexing at the wrist.
2. Hold the bow upright and move the bow left and right like a windshield wiper. Go slowly and feel the bow shift in weight between your index and pinky fingers.
3. Hold the bow upright and crawl your fingers up toward the tip of the bow and back down, returning to a proper bow position.

Revisit the bow exercises periodically to promote a good bow hold and develop an increasingly relaxed bow hand over time.

Holding the Violin

Start by fitting the shoulder rest under the violin, then place the violin on your left shoulder. The scroll of the violin should be slightly higher than horizontal, and the violin should be slanted sideways towards the right slightly. Looking at the violin from straight in front, it should be held at about a 45-degree angle. The word chin rest is somewhat misleading. Your jaw should be on the chin rest, not your chin. Try holding the violin with just your neck and no hands. How does this feel?

Practicing Open String Bowing

Once you have found your bow and violin hold, have a go at playing on each of the open strings. Try to make your bow strokes as long as you can and aim to play on a single string. In the beginning, you may find it challenging to play on one string at a time, but that should gradually become easier. Check that your right shoulder is low when you bow.

Straight Bowing

The bow makes the best sound when it is drawn parallel to the bridge; this is called *straight bowing*. To achieve this, your bow arm should move forward rather than sideways. Imagine a point somewhere in the space in front of you where your hand is going to finish the bow stroke. As you reach the tip of the bow, your arm should be straight in front of you, and as a result, your bow will stay parallel to the bridge, even when playing at the point.

If your bow is slipping away from the bridge and across the fingerboard, you are moving your bow too much to the side. Keep a good grip on the string with your bow to make the string vibrate. If your bow is slipping a lot, it may be because there is too little rosin on the bow.

LESSON 3:
Reading Music

Music is a language that you can read and write. Like any language, music has its own symbols and structure. You learned your native language because you were surrounded by it from birth. If you surround yourself with the language of music, you will become familiar with it over time.

The Staff

Music is organized on a staff of five horizontal lines. It displays virtually all there is to know about a piece of music. Two important things it shows us is how music moves over space and time (rhythm) and how high or low the notes are (pitch). Rhythm is organized horizontally along the staff. Pitch is organized vertically using the lines and spaces. The higher a note's placement, the higher the pitch.

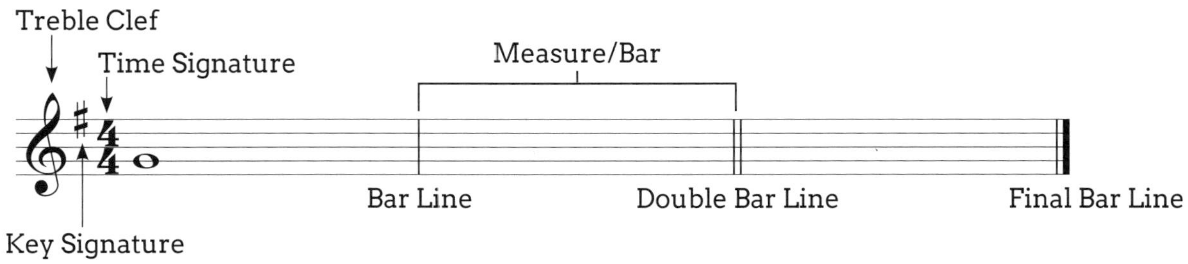

Treble Clef

The treble clef establishes the second line as the note G. The symbol itself is an ornate G, also known as the G Clef. Notice that it curls around the second line to establish G. There are other clefs, but the violin only reads in treble clef.

Around the 12th century, musical scribes gradually began adding a fixed pitch to music notation, usually in the form of a letter at the beginning of each staff. These letters did not have a fixed font, but evolved over time, depending on geographical location and precision in handwriting of the scribe. It wasn't until the 17th century that the treble clef as we know it became standardized.

This: 

Evolved into: 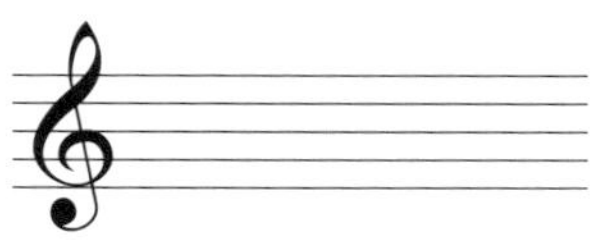

Bar Lines

Bar lines divide the staff into measures. A double bar line is used to mark something significant that occurs in the music, such as a new section. The final bar line is used to mark the end of the song.

Measures

A measure is the space between bar lines. It is also known as a "bar." The movement of music (rhythm) is established from left to right through this space.

Time Signature

The time signature determines how many beats are in each bar and which type of note receives one beat.

Key Signature

The key signature assigns either sharps or flats (never both together) to particular notes for the duration of the song.

The Musical Alphabet

Music notes are alternately written on lines and spaces on the staff. Here is an example:

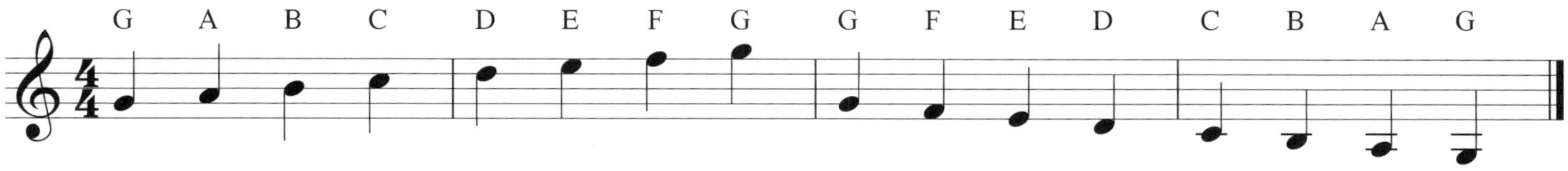

The higher the location of the note on the staff, the higher its pitch.

Each note consists of a note head (the little oval) and a stem. The stem can either be written up or down, depending on the position of the note on the staff. Notes above the center line are written with the stem going down, and notes below the center line have stems going up.

You will have probably noticed from the example above that the notes use the letters of the alphabet from A to G. As the notes are placed higher on the staff, the letter names follow the alphabet up, and as the notes are placed lower on the staff, the alphabet goes in reverse order. It may be helpful to learn to say the alphabet backward from G to A: G-F-E-D-C-B-A.

The note head indicates not only the pitch but also the duration of the note. We will learn about how long each note lasts in more detail as we progress through this course. For now, even as notes may look different, focus on whether the note is positioned on a line or space in the staff.

The names of the violin strings are indicated on the staff as follows:

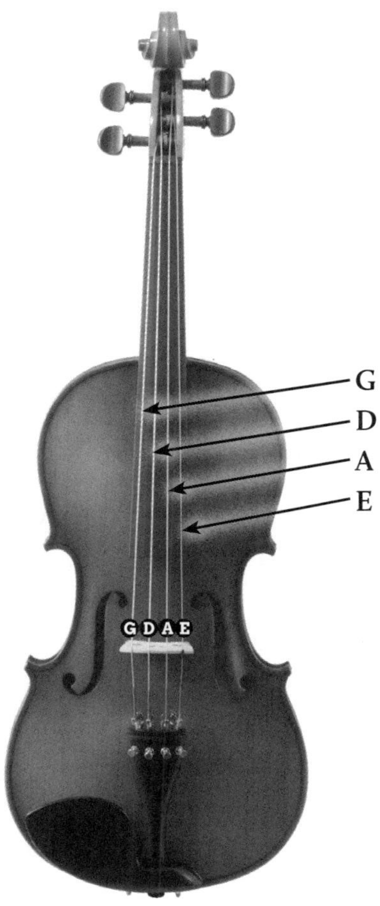

Playing on Open Strings

Let's now pluck each of your violin strings: G D A E. Can you hear that the pitch of the notes is gradually getting higher? Can you sing or hum along while you pluck the strings?

VIOLIN TALK

Musicians on any instrument sing along inside their heads when they play. It is a good habit to get into this at this early stage of your learning so that singing along becomes second nature.

Let's now use the bow and play long notes on the G-string. Bow very slowly and count to four. Use the whole bow from the heel to the point and back. Spread the four counts evenly across the bow so that after two counts you find yourself playing in the middle of the bow. This is called *bow distribution*, and distributing the bow evenly is an important aspect of violin playing.

Playing from the heel of the bow to the point is called playing *down bow*, indicated in music as:

⊓

Playing from the point of the bow to the heel is called playing *up bow*, indicated in music as:

V

Practice alternating down bow and up bow on the G-string, counting to four with each change in bow direction.

In music, this exercise is notated like this:

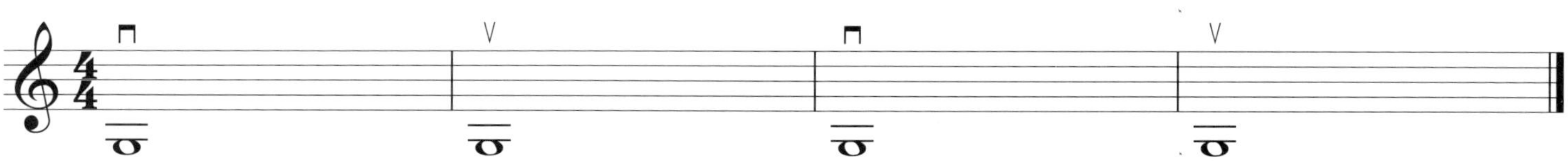

Rhythm

Look at the music example above. Each of these notes on the staff represents one pitch, namely a G. The way the note looks indicates its length. The note used in this music example is called a *whole note*. A whole note is four counts long.

4/4 Time

The numbers at the start of a piece is called a *time signature*. It tells you about the organization of notes in each bar. The top number indicates that there are four counts in one bar. (A bar is a short section of music between two bar lines and groups counts together.) In the case of our example, the bar groups four beats (counts) together. When we play, we count to four.

Playing Long Bows

It is common for violin players to begin a piece of music on a down bow when the piece begins on the first beat of the bar.

When playing a down bow, the bow stroke begins at the heaviest part of the bow. As the playing moves towards the point of the bow, the stick becomes thinner and the bowing naturally lighter, which gives a natural flow to the music. Check out the bowing of an orchestra performing. Can you see all the bows move in the same direction? Orchestral pieces usually finish on a down bow so that all the bows are down at the end of the final note. This looks very neat. In an exuberant piece of music, endings might also end with an up bow, which sounds—and looks—exciting and flashy.

In the following examples there is no bowing indicated, so begin with a down bow.

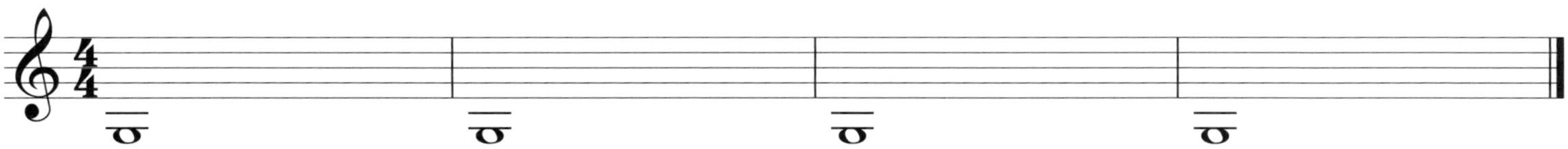

In the next example, let's play on the D-string. Count to four during each note. Use long bows, and make sure that you are in the middle of the bow after two counts.

> **TOOLBOX**
>
> **Repeat Sign**
> The double dots before the final bar line is a repeat sign. Once you reach the end of the music, repeat the section from the beginning.
>
> 

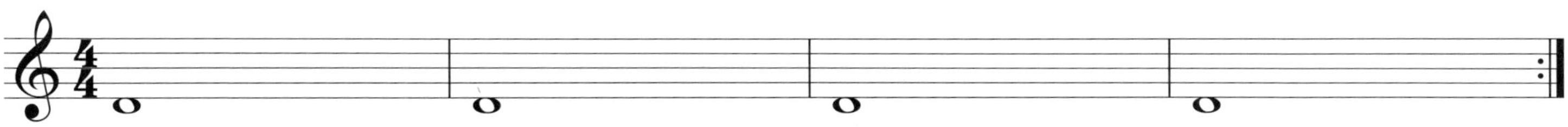

Now practice the same exercise on the A-string while you keep counting 1 2 3 4.

And on the E-string.

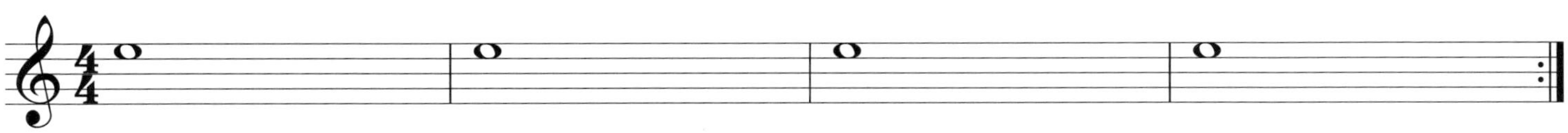

> **VIOLIN TALK**
>
> You will have noticed that playing the violin is multi-tasking! Can you remember to count, use long straight bows, repeat, and sing along in your head, all at the same time?

Playing Songs

Now that you have learned the basics of violin playing, let's apply your knowledge by playing some songs! In the tunes that follow, you will be playing the accompaniment. Play along with the melody on the included audio and video tracks. This will make your playing much more fun. You will also learn to listen and play together, an important skill in making music.

In "Frère Jacques," remember to count in your head and hold each D for four counts. Try to sing the song in your head while you play. The lyrics consist of four syllables: Frè-re Jac-ques. This will help you to keep track of the beat as you play.

Try to leave the bow on the string in between each note and resist the temptation to lift the bow off the string. Violinists leave the bow in contact with the string until the piece has finished. This is called *legato playing*; creating a smooth and flowing sound.

FRÈRE JACQUES **Demo/Backing**

Traditional

Crossing from One String to Another

Elbow Levels

So far, we have played on one string during each piece of music. In this section, we will be learning how to cross from one string to another. We use our right elbow to help us cross from one string to another. The level of your right elbow determines which string you are playing on. Your elbow is in a higher position when playing on the G-string than when you play on the E-string. The video will explain this in more detail.

> **TOOLBOX**
>
> **Whole Rest**
>
> The black rectangle in the music indicates a *whole rest*. Remain silent for four counts, and during that time, lower or raise your right elbow, depending on the note that follows.

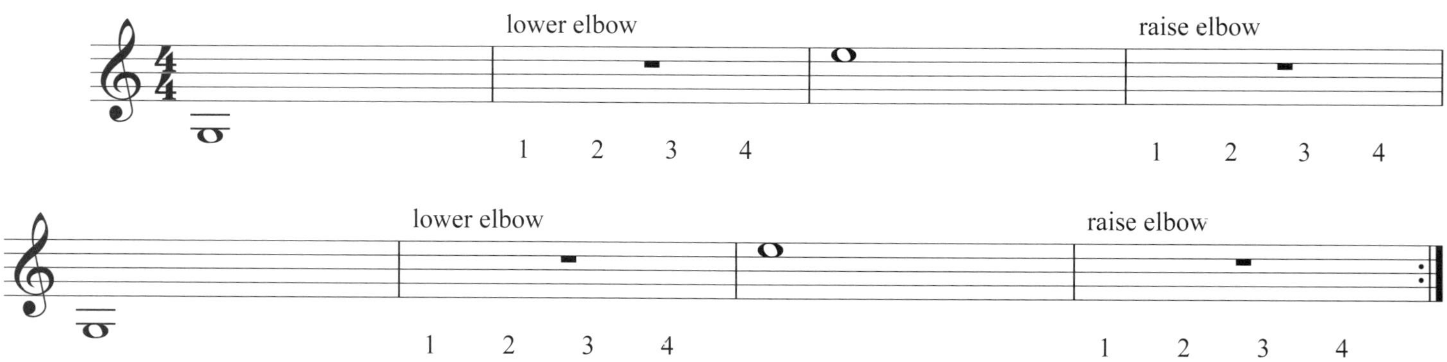

VIOLIN TALK

Even during rests, the bow stays in contact with the string. Leave the bow down while waiting for the next note to begin and roll from one string to the next during the rests. Try not to lift the bow off the string.

Practice these G-D and D-A string crossings.

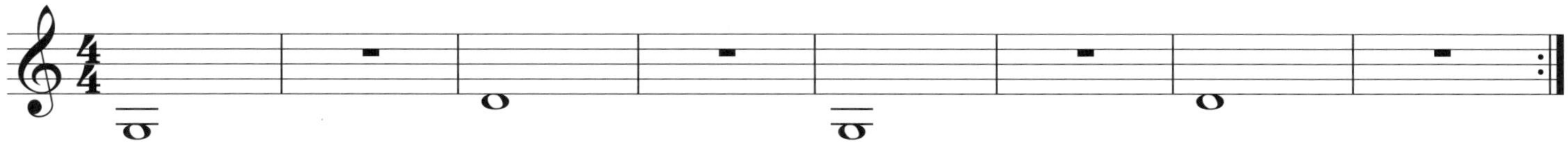

Watch your right elbow in this next exercise! It goes from a lower position to a higher position.

TOOLBOX

Half Note

A *half note* lasts for two counts (half as long as a whole note). Use a whole bow for each of the half notes in "Ode to Joy," thus making the bow travel at twice the speed during the last bar.

"Ode to Joy" is a duet for two violins where you play the open strings G and D. See if you can follow the four beats in each bar and aim to sing the song in your head while you play.

The video lesson will help you practice "Ode to Joy" with the correct technique and will also play the duet with you.

ODE TO JOY Demo/Backing

from SYMPHONY NO. 9 IN D MINOR, FOURTH MOVEMENT CHORAL THEME

Words by Henry van Dyke

Music by Ludwig van Beethoven

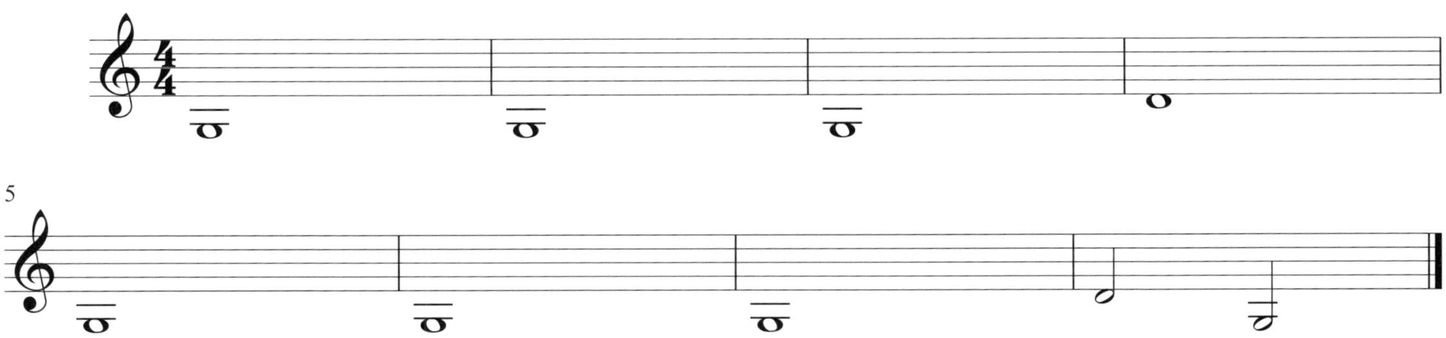

VIOLIN TALK

Always take your time to get ready with a good violin hold, a good bow hold, and your bow ready on the correct string before you start playing.

TOOLBOX

Common Time C

Now that you can cross strings comfortably, let's have another look at time signatures.

So far, we have played in 4/4 which has four beats in a bar. This is also called *common time*, indicated in the music as a **C**. It does not matter if the composer chooses to write the **C** or the 4/4 time signature. The song will sound the same and you will count both in the same way, namely four counts in a bar.

"Twinkle, Twinkle Little Star" is another song with half notes. Use the whole bow for each note. If you hear other strings sounding that you don't mean to play, adjust your elbow level. Watch the video for more about bowing and to play with the accompaniment.

TWINKLE, TWINKLE LITTLE STAR

Demo/Backing

Traditional

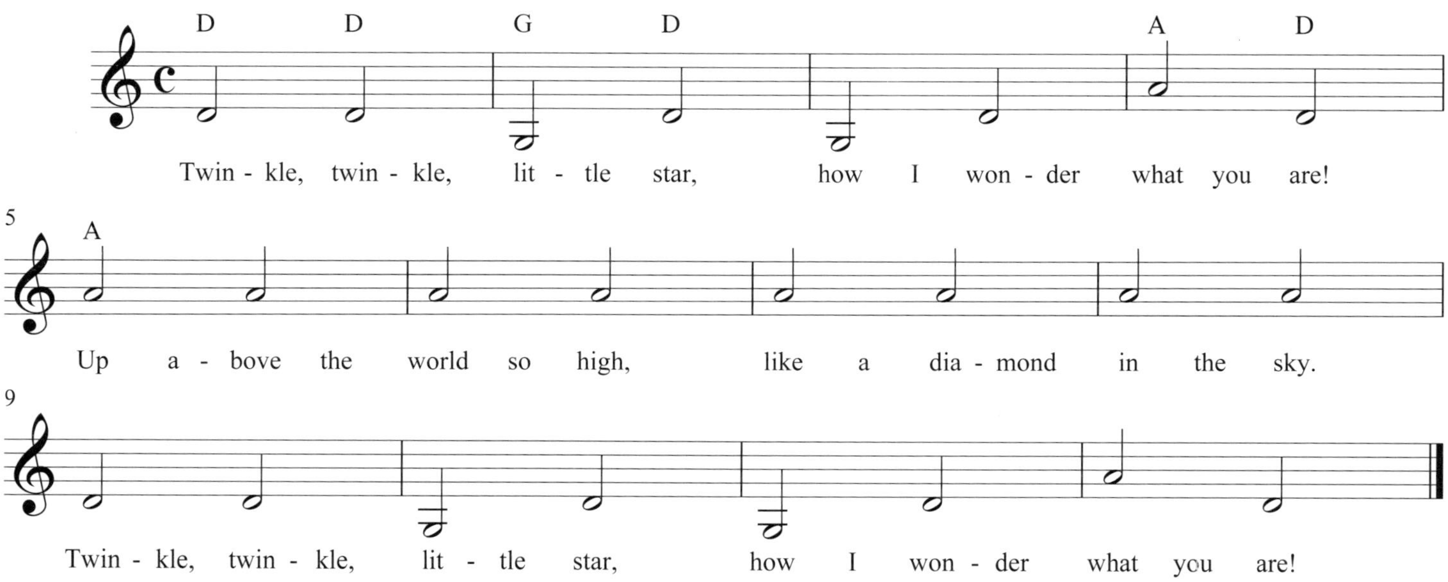

3/4 Time

Next, we will be exploring music in 3/4 time. This means that there are three beats in each bar. We play 3/4 time with a whole bow. Try distributing the bow evenly across all three counts so that each count uses about one-third of the bow.

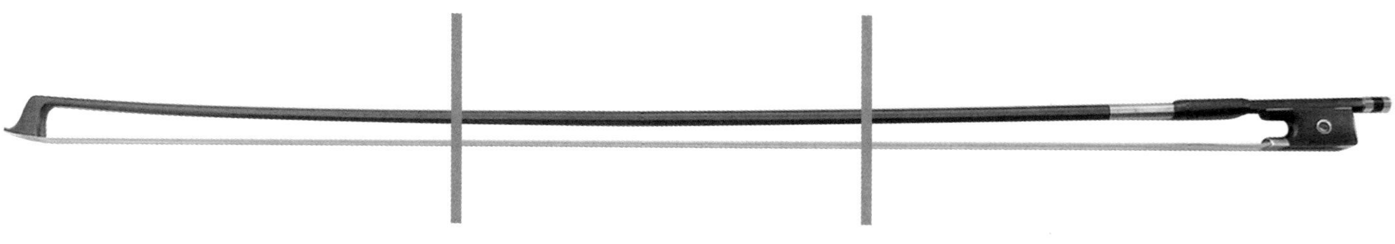

> **TOOLBOX**
>
> **Dotted Notes**
>
> A dot adds half the value of a note's length to the original duration. For example, a half note gets two beats; therefore, a dotted half note is worth three beats (a half note plus a quarter note).
>
> 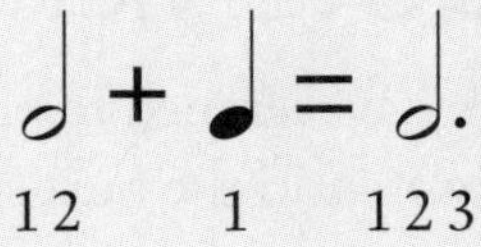
>

LULLABY

By Johannes Brahms

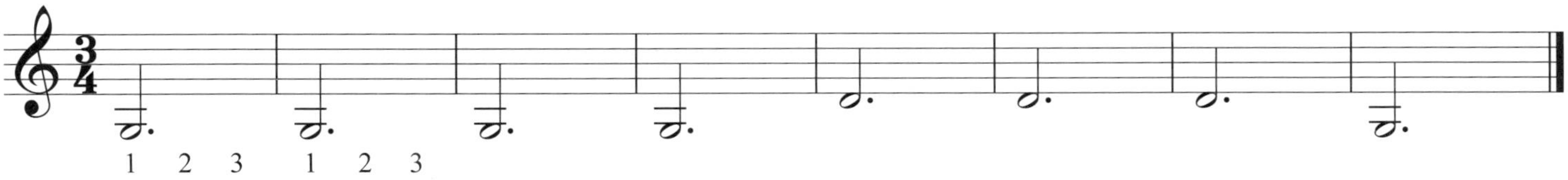

"Kumbaya" is written in 3/4 time, but the melody does not start straight away at the beginning of the song, rather beat 3. When playing with the video, you will have one bar of rest before coming in. The piano will play an accompaniment pattern on beats 1 and 2 and then the melody comes in on beat 3. You will begin playing on beat 1 of the second bar on the on the word "Ya." Sing this song along in your head while you play.

Use the whole bow and let the bow travel slowly from the heel of the bow to the point and back. Note the down bow and up bow signs in the music. Before you begin, place your bow on the G-string at the heel of the bow ready to play.

> **TOOLBOX**
>
> **Quarter Rest**
>
> A *quarter rest* (seen in bar 1) gets one beat of silence.
>
> 

KUMBAYA

Congo Folksong

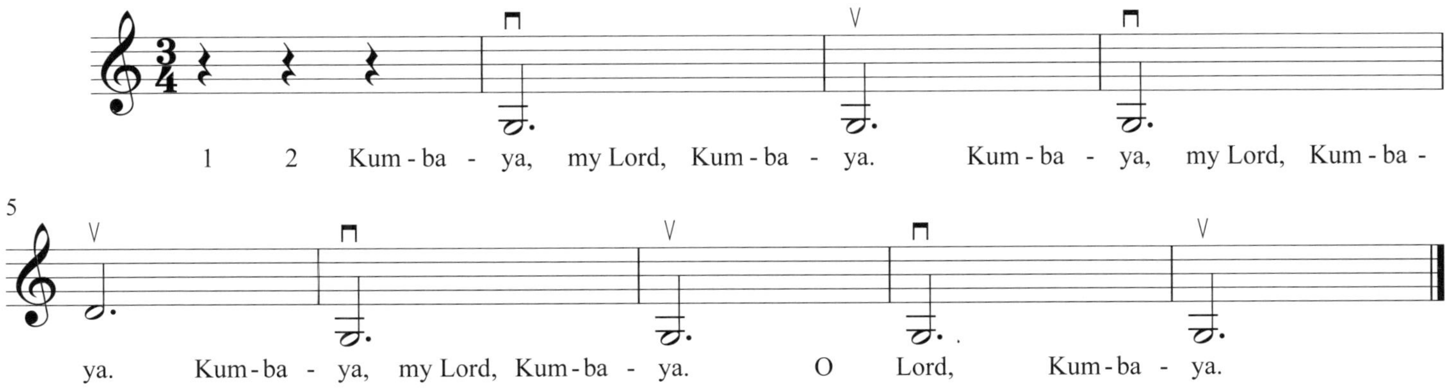

Note Overview

So far, we have learned to play whole notes, half notes, and dotted half notes, and we have used the whole bow for all these notes. In the next section, we will explore quarter notes, which are one count long.

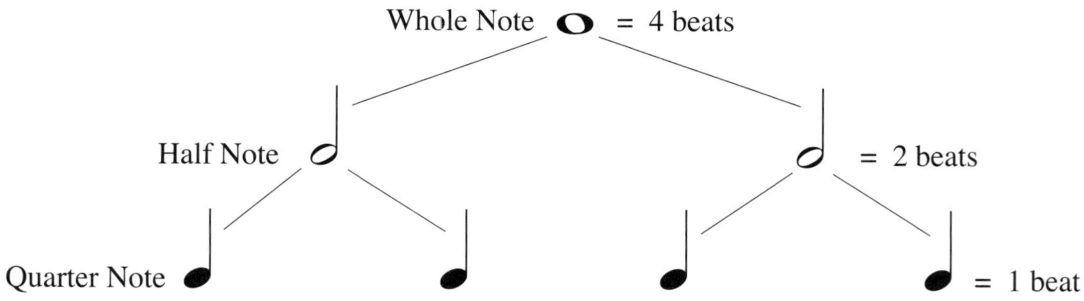

Quarter notes—at this stage—will be played with a half bow, either at the upper half of the bow or at the lower half of the bow. Learning to structure the bowing in this way will organize your playing and help you produce a better sound on the violin. It will take time and practice to become fluent in organizing the bow. We will learn this important aspect of violin playing as we go along.

Playing Short Bows on Quarter Notes

Practice playing short bows at the lower half of the bow. Start playing at the heel of the bow and play each note up to the middle of the bow. Initially, it may be helpful to place a marker in the middle of the bow, such as a sticker, piece of transparent tape, or light pencil line.

Next, practice playing at the upper half of the bow. Start at the point of the bow with an up bow and play to the middle of the bow.

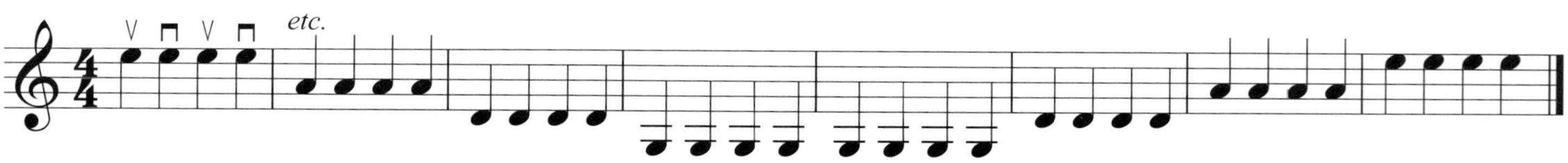

You may notice that a few things are happening now. First, the level of your right elbow changes depending on which string you are playing. Second, you may want to review your bow hold at this point. When you play at the lower half of the bow, there is much more pressure on the pinky of your right hand. Over time, your pinky will become stronger and this will get easier.

VIOLIN TALK

Check your bow hold each time you pick up your bow. This will help you improve your bow hold every day.

Milestone 1

Well done! Wonderful work so far. This is the first milestone on your journey. If you have found the start of your playing quite challenging, that's okay. Give yourself time to grow into all the techniques that you have learned and go over some or all the exercises again until you have mastered the techniques before you carry on.

LESSON 4:
The Left Hand

Left-Hand Position

Now that you have made good progress with your bow, it is time to learn to use the left hand.

- Draw a line near the base of your index finger at the crease.
- Place the violin on your shoulder and use the finger line to create a "V" between the base of the E-string and your finger line. This determines the height of your fingers above the string, where your bottom knuckles will be level with the strings.

- Place your hand as far back as you can manage.
- Your thumb should be upright, just peeking over the edge about half a nail above the fingerboard.
- Your left wrist should be a relatively straight line and not bent forward or pushed out. There should be about the space of a tennis ball between your wrist and the body of the violin.
- Your left elbow should be under the body of the violin.

Correct:

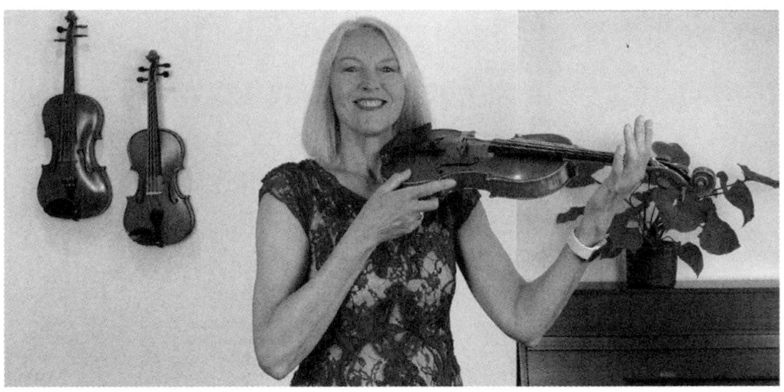

Incorrect:

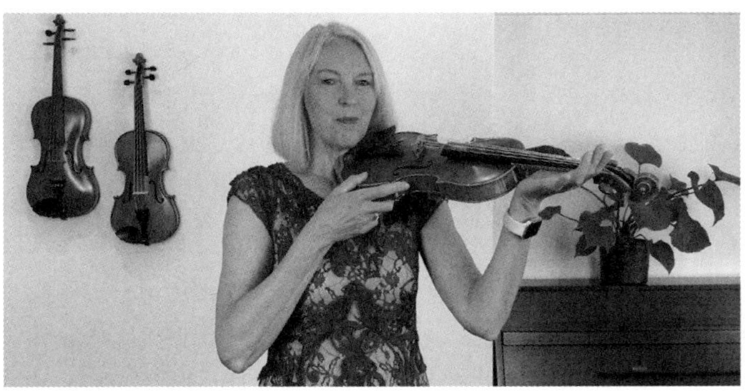

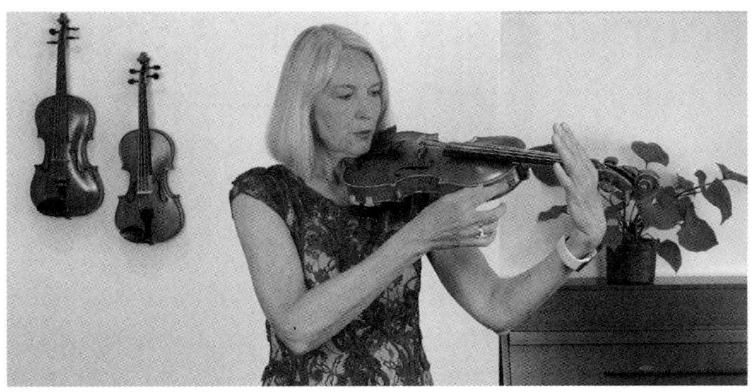

Watch the video to get a good foundation of the left-hand position.

Left-Hand Plucking Exercise

Bring your hand up the violin, then lift your hand high above the strings and bring your pinky toward the G-string. Pluck the G-string with your pinky. You'll feel a stretch between your shoulder and upper arm. If you can't reach, try bringing your elbow further under the violin. Next, practice the D-string with your ring finger, the A-string with your middle finger, and the E-string with your index finger.

The left-hand position will only work effectively if the violin is positioned properly on your shoulder. If you have not yet obtained a shoulder rest, now is the time to start playing with one. Ultimately, you will need to be able to hold the violin with your neck muscles so that the left hand can play independently without having to support the violin. Holding the violin is a balance between the neck and the left hand, so when you need to focus on the left-hand fingers, the neck can support the violin more, and when your neck gets tired, your left hand will do some of the work.

Playing Fingers on the A-String

Each time before playing with left-hand fingers on a string, take a moment to check over the position of the left hand. This will help you get used to the correct playing position more quickly. More importantly, it will help you to play in tune if the fingers are positioned properly from the start.

Stick your index finger up into the air and practice rolling it up and down. When closed, there should be no space between the two joints of your finger. Press the string down with the pad of your finger (you may need to cut your nails). When not playing on a string, hover your fingers just above the string.

Play your open A and while playing, sing the next note B, in your head. Fold up your finger completely and place it on the string about a finger width away from the nut. If the note doesn't sound correct, lift your finger, and try placing it in a slightly different spot. It may take a couple of tries to find the correct position. Watch the video to see this technique in greater detail.

Four Fingers on the A-String

In the following music examples, the fingering is written above the notes, and the letter names of the notes are written underneath. As you go along, try to memorize the letter names of the notes. The C♯ is called a C-sharp. Later, you will learn why we call this note C-sharp, and why the other notes are just called A, B, and so on. For now, we will focus on learning to play.

To start, you will always place your fingers in a specific pattern. Fingers one (index finger) and two (middle finger) have a space between them, fingers two and three (ring finger) are close together, and fingers three and four (pinky) have a gap. This pattern is an important aid in learning to play in tune. Bear in mind that the first finger is also approximately a finger width away from the nut.

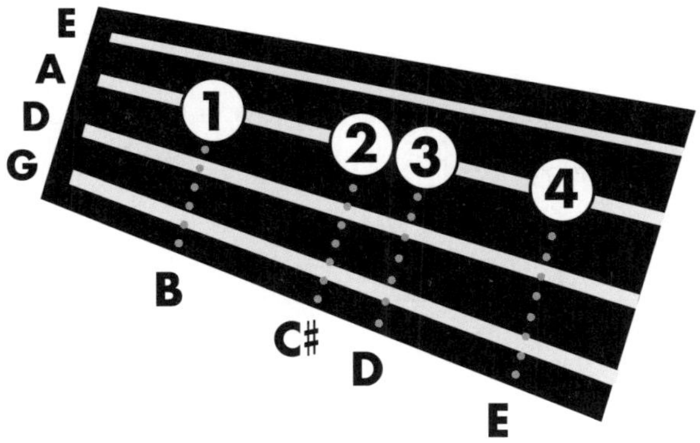

We can also indicate the pattern like this (the hyphen indicates the space between the fingers):

0-1-23-4

You may have noticed that the fourth finger on the A-string is the same note as the open E-string. We are playing this note with a fourth finger here to practice using the little finger and make it stronger.

Play with round fingers and on your fingertips as much as you can. Leave each finger down on the string once you have played it, adding fingers as you play 0-1-23-4. By the time you get to the fourth finger, you should have all four fingers on the string. Try to keep your left thumb upright and soft, and opposite your index finger. This should keep your wrist straight and will help direct your fingers toward the fingerboard and not in the air. Any finger that you are not playing is hovering above the fingerboard.

If you find that your fingers collapse and become flat rather than round, it may be that you are pressing too hard. You only need to press the string down so that the string is stopped on the fingerboard. Any more pressure that you apply will hurt your fingers and will not add any value to your playing. As we have seen in previous lessons, it will take time to develop stamina so that you can hold the violin for longer periods.

VIOLIN TALK

Practice for short bursts of time and come back to playing the violin often. This will help you develop a good technique, strengthen your fingers, and aid concentration. Playing three times for ten minutes will be far more effective at this stage than playing for half an hour in one go.

TOOLBOX

Accidentals

♭ **FLAT** Lowers a note one half-step

♯ **SHARP** Raises a note one half-step

♮ **NATURAL** Cancels a sharp or flat

An *accidental* is a sharp, flat, or natural sign that appears in music. Accidentals are good for an entire measure. For example, in the next exercise, you see a sharp symbol before the C, making it a C♯. The following note is also a C♯ because the accidental applies to all notes in the measure.

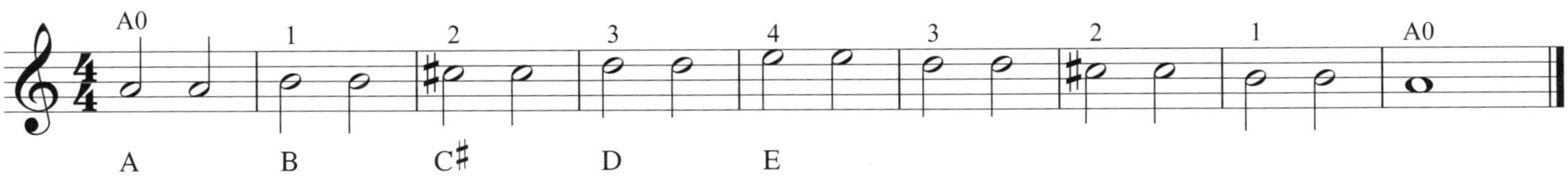

Four Fingers on the D-String

Once you have mastered playing the notes on the A-string, have a go at playing notes on the D-string. Play very slowly and try to use a whole bow for each of the notes.

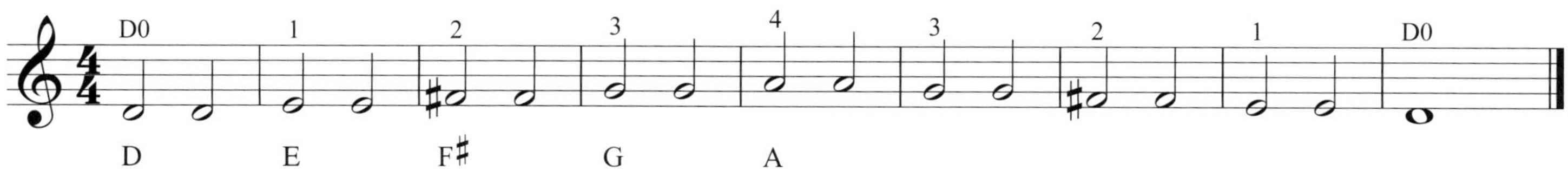

The D Scale

Next, we are going to expand our range of notes and learn a D scale. A *scale* is a sequence of eight notes that go up by step and then down again. In the case of the D scale, we play from a low D to a high D. At the top, we ornament the high D with a little practice of the fourth finger before going down again to the low D. Learning to play scales improves the fluency and accuracy of our notes.

TOOLBOX

Key Signature

A *key signature* indicates whether to play a note sharp, flat, or natural. Sharp (♯) or flat (♭) signs are placed after the treble clef. The line or space that the sharp or flat occupies indicates which notes are changed.

For now, we will focus only on sharps. The two sharps we have in the example below are F♯ and C♯.

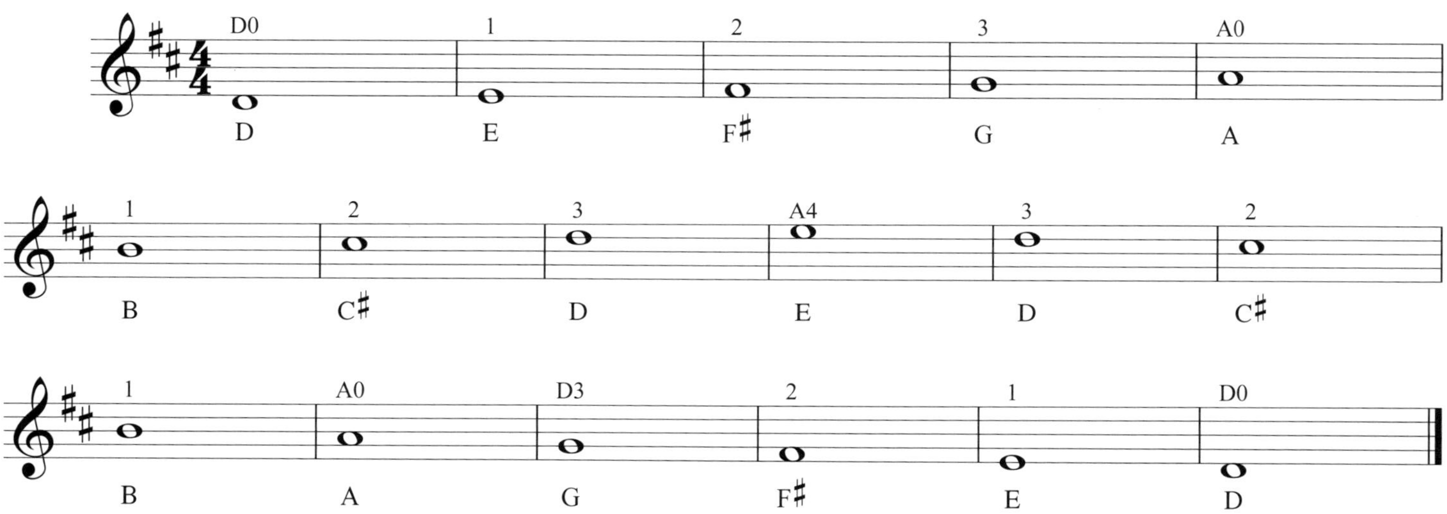

When you play this scale, listen carefully to the tuning of each note. Remember, your finger pattern is the starting point, but from there you will need to fine-tune your fingers to play the notes perfectly in tune. Playing the scale with the video will help you play even better in tune because you can relate your own pitch on your violin to the pitch of the accompaniment. Remember that singing the scale in your head will also help with your intonation.

VIOLIN TALK

Make a habit of singing along in your head. Ideally, you sing the note before you even start playing it so that you always anticipate how a note will sound in advance.

The A Scale

The A scale starts on the open A-string and continues upward until you have reached the fourth finger on the E-string before going down the scale.

You will surely spot the time signature, 4/4 time. We are now playing four quarter notes in each bar. Start down bow and play each note at the lower half of the bow. In the last bar of the scale there is a whole note. Hold this last note for four counts and play with a very slow, long bow.

VIOLIN TALK

If you haven't already done so, now is the time to memorize the letter names of the notes on the D-, A-, and E-strings.

Tuning the Third Fingers with Open Strings

As an extra review of the tuning of the third fingers, we can check the notes with the open string below it. Remember that the third finger on the D-string is called G. Therefore, this G should match with the open G-string. Likewise, the third finger on the A-string is called D, so it can be checked with the open D-string.

TOOLBOX

FORWARD REPEAT SIGN

When playing through music, make a mental note when you see a forward repeat sign. Once you reach an end repeat sign, instead of returning to the beginning of the music, go back to the start of the forward repeat sign.

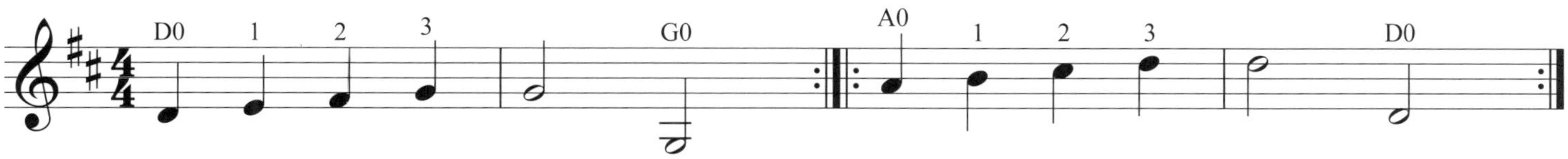

The G Scale

If you can play a D and A scale, you will find the G scale quite straightforward. Whilst the notes and the left-hand fingers will gradually have become more manageable to play, in this scale, we will develop our bowing by combining half notes and quarter notes. Use a whole bow for each half note and a half bow for each quarter note. The quarter notes are played first at the upper half and then at the lower half. At the end of the scale, play the whole note with a very slow, whole bow.

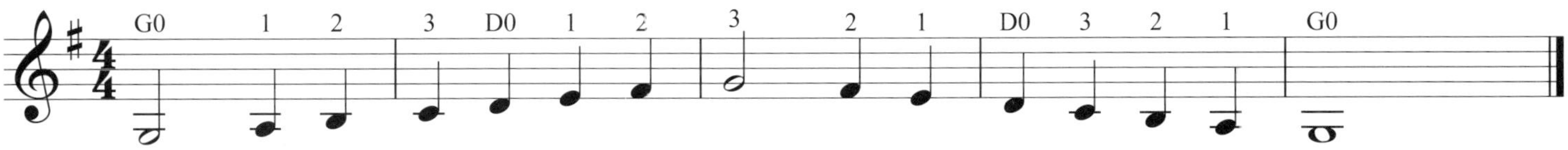

In the next piece, we are using the notes from the D major scale therefore we are playing in the key of D major. Note that the key signature has two sharps. This is a feature of the D major scale. There is also a repeat at the end.

AU CLAIR DE LA LUNE

French Folksong

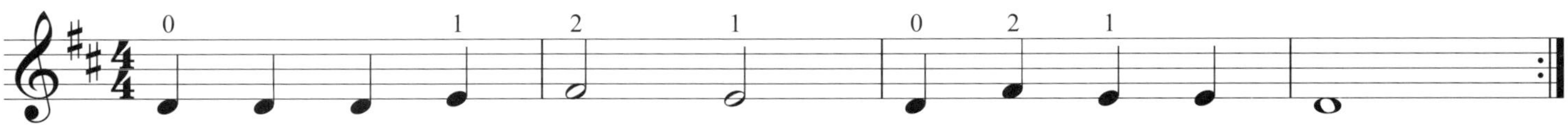

Can you also play "Au Clair de la Lune" on the A-string? What about on the G- and E-strings?

Eighth Notes

Let's look at some faster notes, *eighth notes*. Eighth notes receive half a beat of sound, making them twice as fast as quarter notes. To count eighth notes, we must subdivide the beat. We use the word "and" (represented in the music as "+") to do this. So, a group of eighth notes would be counted as "one-and-two-and-three-and-four-and."

Eighth notes on their own look like this:

However, very often two eighth notes are beamed together, which makes reading the notes much easier:

VIOLIN TALK

It makes sense to count a piece through before playing it. That way, you are better prepared and will learn faster.

When we play eighth notes, we use shorter, quarter bows. Normally we use half bows for quarter notes; however, in bar 4, we need to use a long bow for the quarter note on beat one. This is so that when we reach the half note on beat three, we can use a whole bow. Use this technique for all circled measures in the music.

Watch the video for a more detailed explanation of how the notes fit on the bow. Start the song with a down bow at the heel of the bow.

BAA BAA BLACK SHEEP

Traditional

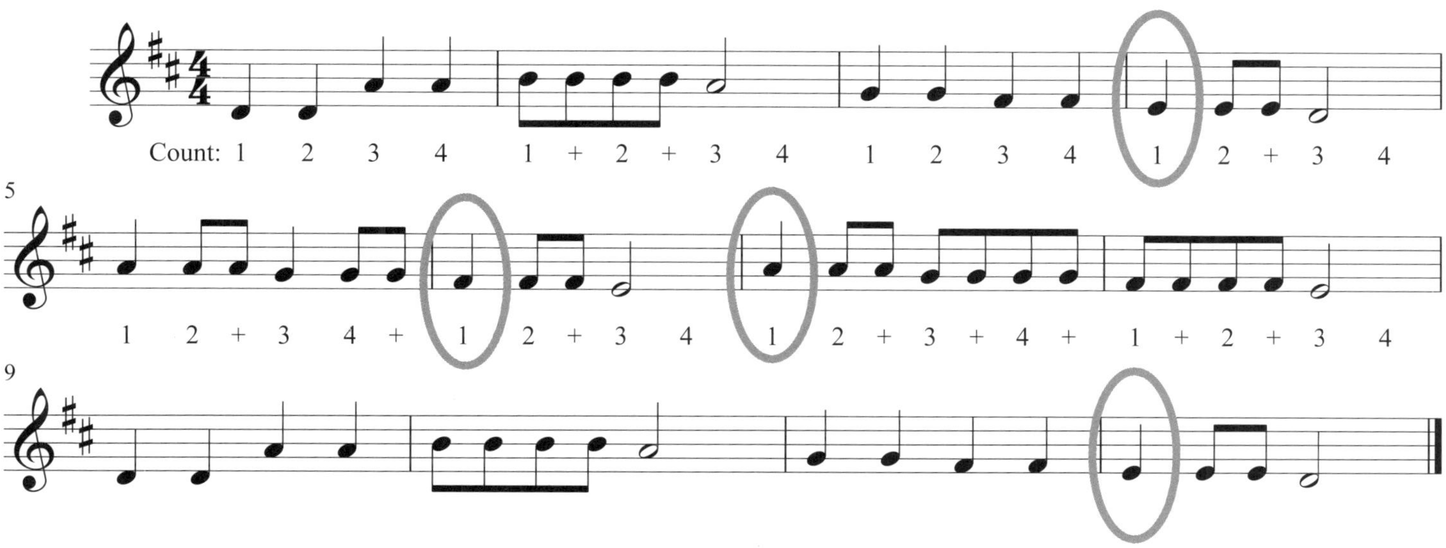

Rests

Just as different notes indicate different lengths of sounds, *rests* indicate different lengths of silence. We have already come across the whole rest in *Crossing from One String to Another* and the quarter rest in "Kumbaya." Here is an overview of all the notes and their equivalent rests.

Whole Note	4 beats	𝅝	Whole Rest	𝄻
Half Note	2 beats	𝅗𝅥	Half Rest	𝄼
Quarter Note	1 beat	♩	Quarter Rest	𝄽
Eighth Note	½ beat	♪	Eighth Rest	𝄾

Before you begin playing "We Will Rock You," prepare your fingers on the D-string. This is indicated by the small notes at the start of the music. Take your time to place each finger perfectly in tune. Once you have found your third finger, test it with the open G-string. As you know, the third finger on the D-string is called G, so they should match in tuning. When you have rests, place your fingers on the D-string again so you are ready and waiting before you play the next section.

Now have a look at the rests in this music; there are two bars of whole note rests at the end of each passage. Count these out while you play. Some bars have a quarter rest followed by a half rest. In these bars you count:

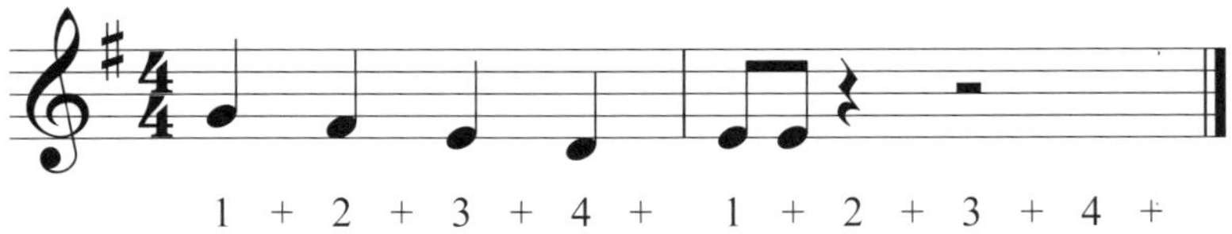

WE WILL ROCK YOU

Demo/Backing

Words and Music by Brian May

VIOLIN TALK

Before playing, always check your bow hold, violin position, left hand, and starting note.

Here are some tips for playing "Can Can." As always, watch the video for further instruction on how to play this tune.

- To finger the G in bar 1, add both your second and third fingers. That way you're able to easily play down the scale in the notes following. This is referred to as *secondary finger action*, where you are moving a finger early to prepare for something later in the music.
- In bar 4, you have a D major scale—something you're already familiar with. Use the same technique of placing all three of your fingers on the string at the same time.
- In the last bar, you can use a fourth finger or open string to play the A.
- Use a whole bow for the quarter notes and half note, and a half bow for the eighth notes.

CAN CAN

from ORPHEUS IN THE UNDERWORLD

By Jacques Offenbach

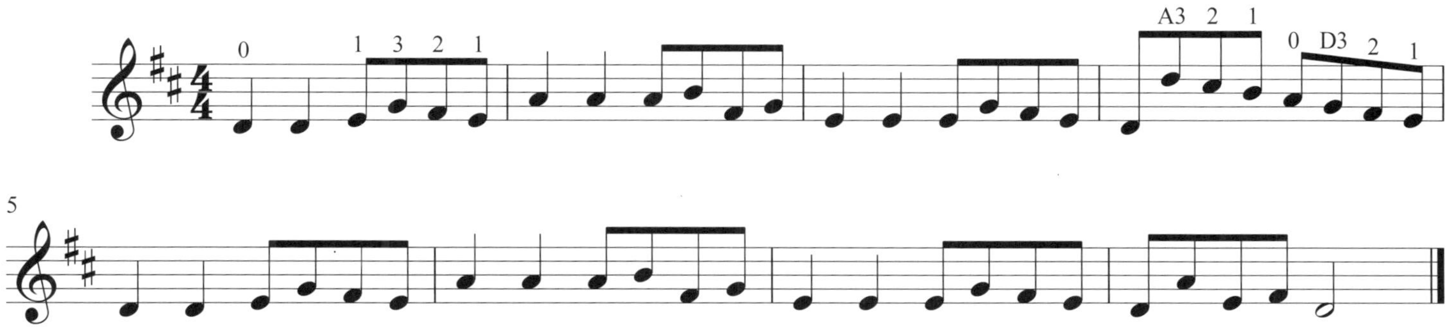

The D and A Major Arpeggio

An *arpeggio* is a kind of short version of a scale. We are learning scales and arpeggios because they appear—either in full or in part—frequently in many pieces of music. You should aim to memorize the scales and arpeggios as you come across them. If you learn to spot them in your music, sight reading becomes second nature, and learning new pieces of music will take less time and effort.

Play the arpeggios slowly with long bows so that you can work on producing a beautiful tone. Remember to play with a straight bow.

D Major Arpeggio

A Major Arpeggio

LESSON 5:

Bow Control

Zig-Zag Bowing

So far, all the bowings that we have practiced have been evenly spread on the bow. However, when we play in 3/4 time, we can't share the notes evenly, as there is an odd number of notes. Instead, we have to zig-zag the bow to get from the point to the heel, or from the heel to the point.

In *zig-zag bowing*, the middle note will use less bow and travels more slowly across the string than the first and third notes. Despite the difference in bow length, we should not hear a difference in sound. In the next example, use zig-zag bowing on each bar with three quarter notes. These are indicated with a zig-zag line.

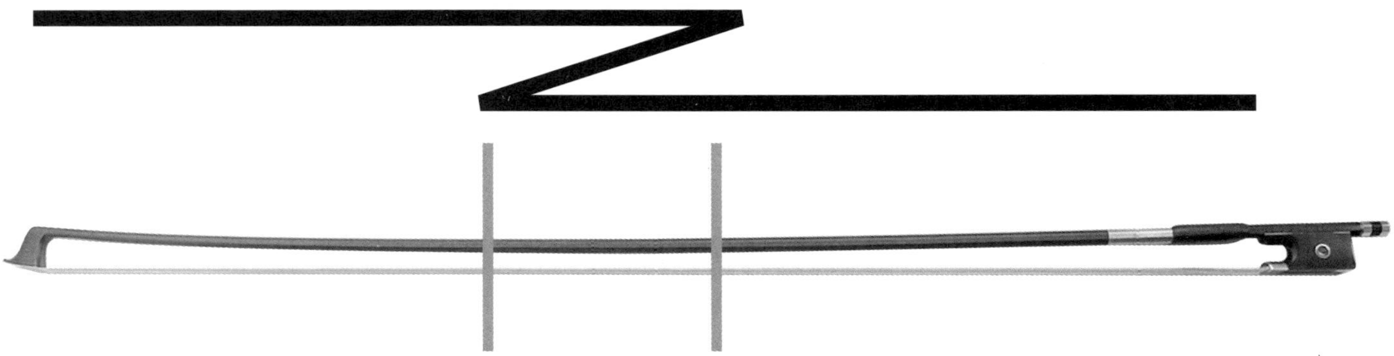

TOOLBOX

Tie

A *tie* is a curved line connecting notes of the same pitch. Play one note for the combined counts of the tied notes. For example, a dotted half note tied to a quarter note is held for four beats.

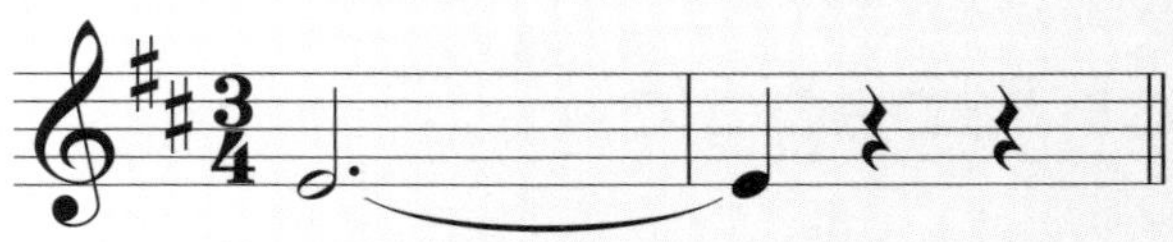

MORNING HAS BROKEN

Words by Eleanor Farjeon
Music by Cat Stevens

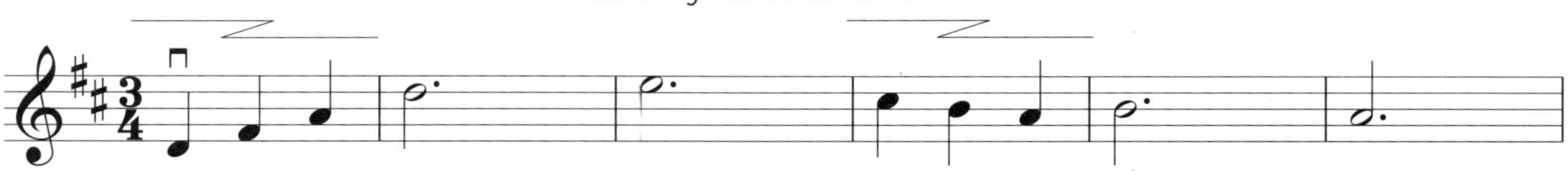

TOOLBOX

Look for Patterns

Notice how sections of the D and A major scales and arpeggios appear in "Morning Has Broken." When playing a new piece, try to find out if there are any scale or arpeggio patterns. Spotting these patterns will improve your playing.

Playing Slurs

When we play more than one note on a single bow stroke, we are slurring notes. Let's practice playing two open strings on one bow. Try to change notes when you approach the middle of the bow. The marker in the middle of the bow that you had on your bow previously might be helpful for this exercise too. Make the string crossings with your right elbow, just like you practiced in Lesson 3.

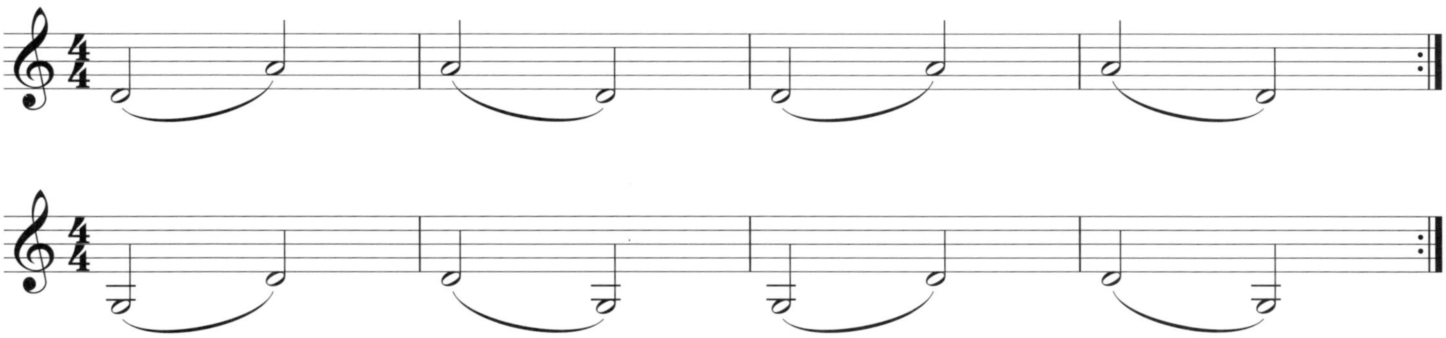

We can also slur notes from a higher string to a lower string. When you slur from a higher string to a lower string, your elbow will move up.

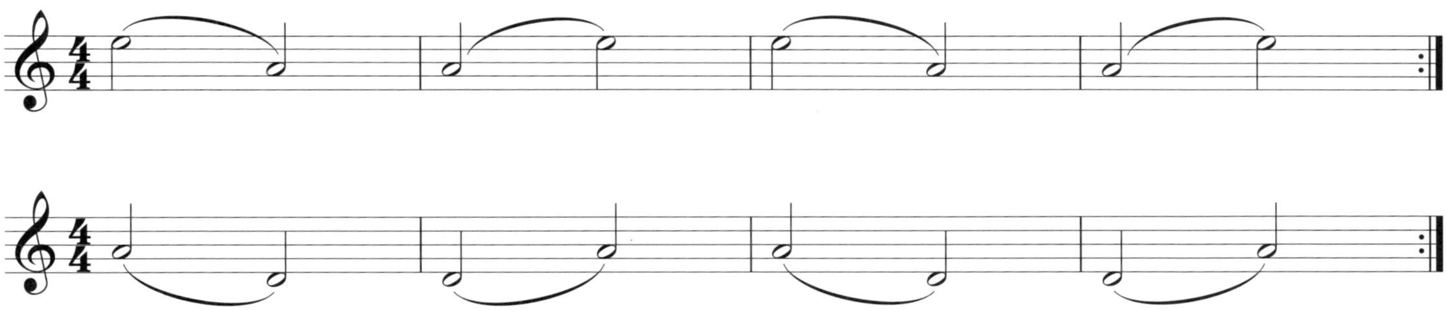

Slurring Using Fingers

Next, let's practice slurs that use fingers. Again, make sure that you change notes in the middle of the bow. Have your left hand finger on the string, ready to play before you begin.

Slurred Scale Passage

We will make slurring a bit more challenging now. Can you slur three notes on one bow?

Remember to divide the bow into three even sections and use the whole bow, starting at the heel of the bow. In order to articulate notes clearly when slurring, tap your fingers harder as you place them on the fingerboard. When you take your fingers away, move them in a quick, rapid movement.

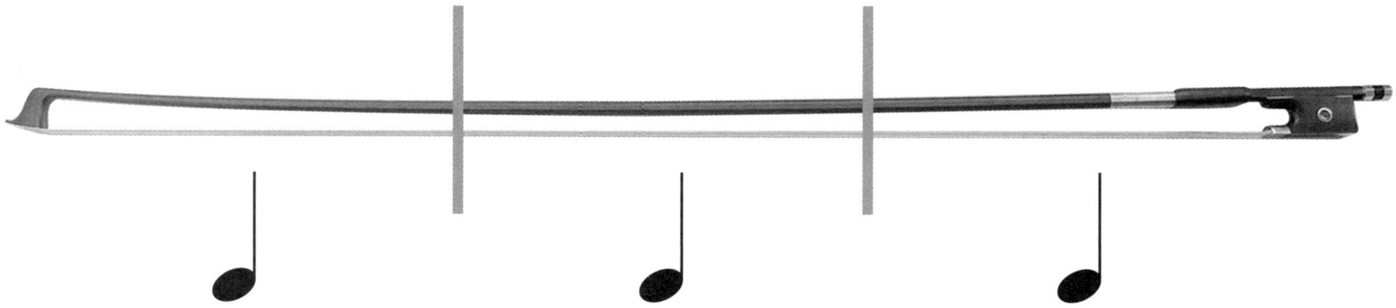

Next, let's try slurring the arpeggio patterns in "Morning Has Broken." Remember to tap your fingers when moving between notes as we did in the previous example. Many beginners will try to articulate the up bow in bar 2 by accenting with the bow hand. Resist this urge; good articulation comes from how you place your left-hand fingers on the fingerboard.

In bar 10, all the notes can be played on the D-string using your fourth finger for the A. This will make your playing softer and gentler. In bar 11, your bow should travel more slowly as the note is held for 4 counts.

MORNING HAS BROKEN

Words by Eleanor Farjeon
Music by Cat Stevens

You may have noticed that when you play "Morning Has Broken" with slurs, the music sounds more even and controlled, which adds to the expressiveness of your performance. It is also easier to play with the bow as the bow strokes all have the same length, and you play each bar with a whole bow.

Dotted Rhythms

We already know that a dot after a note means we add half the note value to it. For a *dotted quarter note*, we divide the quarter note into two eighth notes and then add another eighth note. A dotted quarter note lasts for three eighth notes and we will count it "1-and-2."

$1\frac{1}{2} = 1 + \frac{1}{2}$

When we play a dotted quarter note, the bow will be very uneven on the single eighth note. Be careful not to play too loudly on the short note as the main emphasis of the music is always on the first beat of the bar.

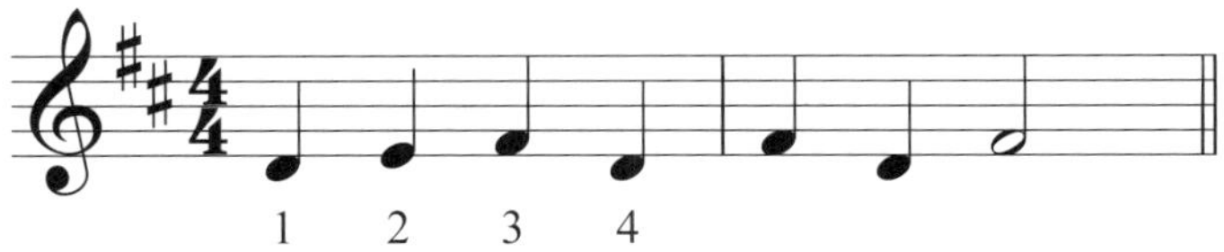

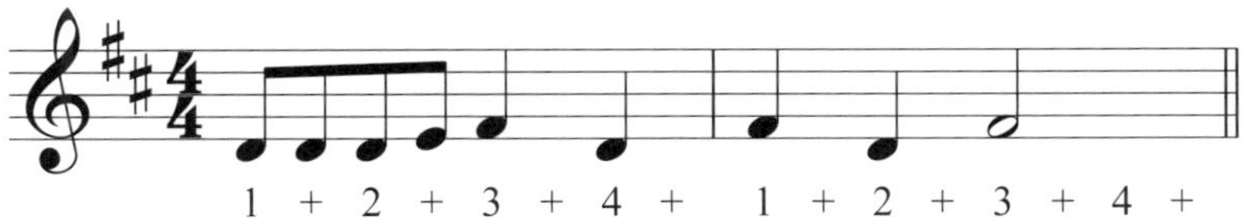

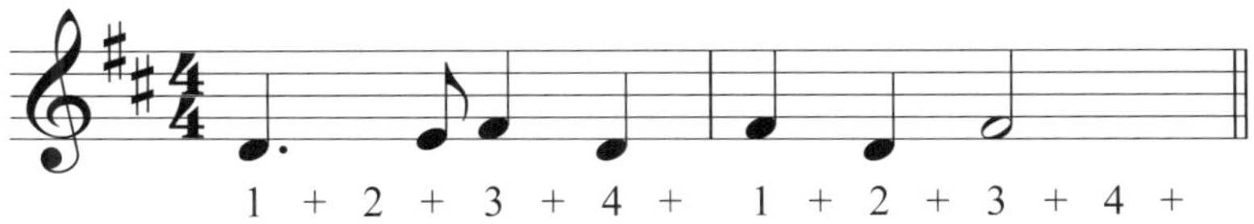

Practicing Do-Re-Mi

When you first learn to play "Do-Re-Mi," play very slowly and count out all the dotted rhythms. It is important to listen to the timing of the eighth notes. Are your bow and left hand perfectly synchronized?

There are a couple of places where we play notes that are five notes apart, such as bar 9. This is called a perfect 5th and it is an important skill to be able to recognize this sound as our strings are tuned in 5ths. In bars 11 and 13, there is another perfect 5th played on two different strings. When this occurs, do not hop your finger from one string to another; instead, place your finger in between the two strings.

Look at bar 14. If you know the song, you probably know how to play this rhythm. Can you work out how to count it?

The bowing is uneven, so stay at the lower half of the bow until you reach the half note in bar 2. This note is played with a whole bow, which brings you to the point of the bow. Stay at the upper half in bar 3, as you have a whole note in bar 4, which needs a whole bow. As you become more experienced, bowing will become more automatic, but at this stage, it is a good habit to work out how you will be bowing a piece.

VIOLIN TALK

Bow organization is an important aspect of violin playing. Taking a few minutes to decide how to bow a piece will improve your tone considerably.

DO-RE-MI Demo/Backing

from THE SOUND OF MUSIC

Lyrics by Oscar Hammerstein II
Music by Richard Rodgers

Fourth Fingers Versus Open Strings

We know that the fourth finger on a string is the same pitch as the open string above, but the *timbre* (quality) of the note is very different. In this early stage of playing, we practiced the fourth finger for strength and used the open string for ease of playing. In advanced playing, we use the fourth finger and open strings depending on the musical effect we would like to achieve.

As a rule, use the fourth finger when the following note is on a lower string, and use an open string when the following note is on a higher string. However, you probably spotted in "Do-Re-Mi" that you can get away with using the open A-string at the start of bar 9.

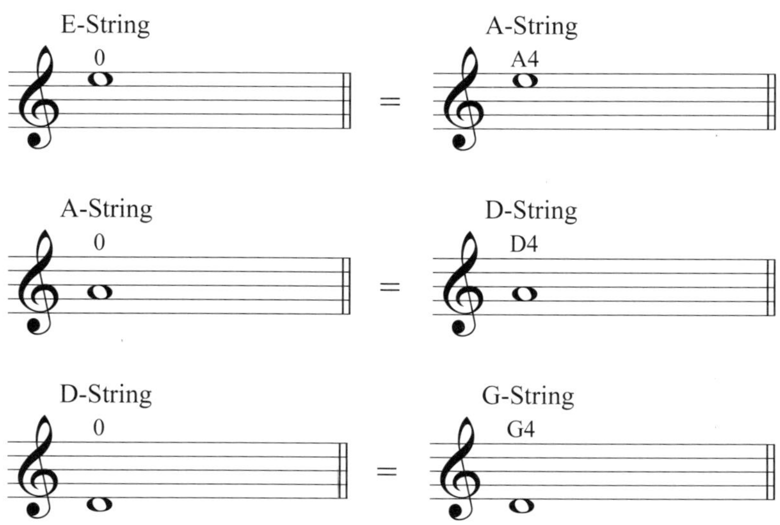

Practicing Ode to Joy

Think carefully about the organization of the bow.

- Play the quarter notes in the first two lines at the lower half of the bow.
- The B in bar 9 (whole bow) takes you to the upper half of the bow.
- The E in bar 12 should be played with a whole bow so that you can play the tied note in bars 12-13 with a long bow.
- Play the last note in bar 15 with a whole bow to make space for the long bows in bar 16.

ODE TO JOY

from SYMPHONY NO. 9 IN D MINOR, FOURTH MOVEMENT CHORAL THEME

Words by Henry van Dyke
Music by Ludwig van Beethoven

Practicing We Wish You a Merry Christmas

In "We Wish You a Merry Christmas," we are playing in 3/4 time. We know that the bowing is uneven in 3/4 time. Use a generous amount of bow around the middle to make the bowing work here.

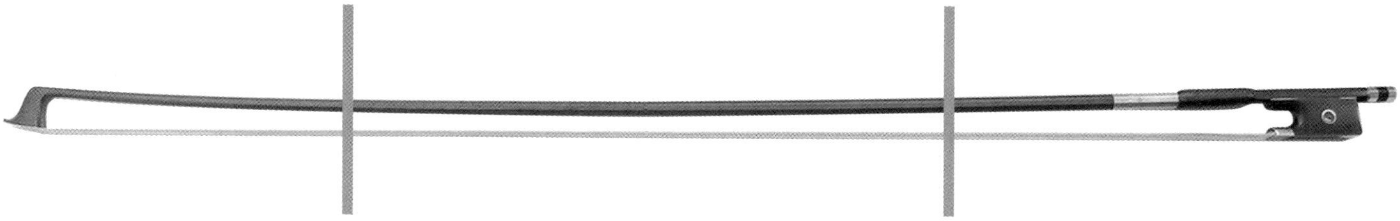

You can practice playing open strings and fourth fingers in "We Wish You a Merry Christmas" too. Use your fourth finger when you stay on the same string for the note before and after. When the note after the open string is on that string (bar 3), play the open A-string.

Also be aware that when you play the C with the second finger on the A-string in bar 5, your second finger falls right beside the first finger. (More later on why.)

> **TOOLBOX**
>
> **Upbeat**
>
> An *upbeat* (or *pickup*) is a musical phrase that starts before the beat with the main emphasis, the first beat of the following bar. Upbeats are usually played up bow.

"We Wish You a Merry Christmas" starts on beat 3 of the imaginary first bar; it starts with an upbeat. Note the up bow sign at the start. The main emphasis in the first phrase is on the word "wish." This should be played with a down bow. Down bows go with gravity and are naturally slightly stronger than up bows.

The lyrics have been added at the beginning of the song to help you associate how the notes relate to the lyrics of this popular tune.

WE WISH YOU A MERRY CHRISTMAS

Traditional English Folksong

Practicing When the Saints Go Marching In

In this piece, we will *re-take* the bow. This means that after the half note, we re-set the bow to the place where we started at the beginning of the song. Each new up bow is played at the same place and will therefore sound the same as every other up bow. This will make the piece more even in sound since all the bowings are the same.

Start with an up bow in the middle of the bow so that you are at the heel of the bow when you play the half note A. Re-take the bow back to the middle during the rest so that the second set of eighth notes also start in the middle of the bow. In bar 6, stay at the upper half of the bow and play the eighth notes at the end of bar 7 as you played these at the start of the piece.

WHEN THE SAINTS GO MARCHING IN

Traditional

Practicing London Bridge Is Falling Down

Remember, a tie in the music means to hold the note for its combined value. Hold the last note for three and a half counts. You count this "1 and-2-3-4." Note that the F♯ and the D are also slurred notes.

LONDON BRIDGE IS FALLING DOWN

Traditional

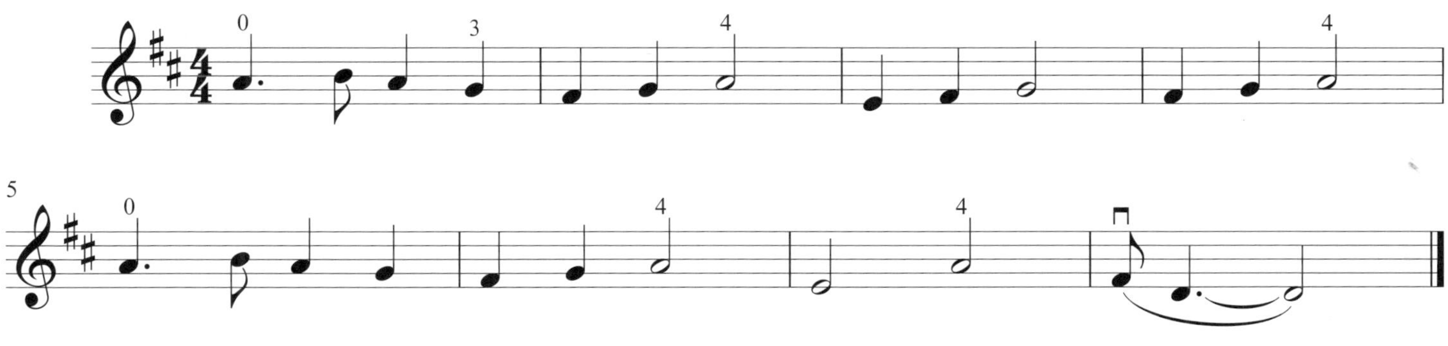

More Bow Control

Bow control is the essence of violin playing. As violin players, we are always aiming to improve our bow control. Try these exercises to continue improving your bow control:

1. On an open string, alternate playing a down bow at the point and up bow at the heel. Go slowly and try to control the bow so it's not bouncing when you place it on the string.
2. With a proper bow hold, roll the bow forward and back between your fingers. You'll notice the bow rolls between the tip and middle of your thumb. After a couple of rolls, check that you still have the correct bow hold.

Practicing Auld Lang Syne

- This piece is in 4/4 time. Every quarter note is one count. When there are eighth notes, use the word "and" to subdivide the beat. Note that the counting is written below the notes and the fingering is written above.
- This piece is constituted of 4-bar phrases and each of these phrases starts with an upbeat.
- Play up bows where they are marked in the music.
- On the dotted half notes, use a whole bow and bow very slowly to "save the bow."

AULD LANG SYNE

Words by Robert Burns
Traditional Scottish Melody

Milestone 2

Well done! You can play more challenging pieces with dotted rhythms and more complicated bowing.

LESSON 6:
Notes on the G- and E-String

Notes on the G-String

It is easy to forget the notes on the G-string; that's why we are practicing them here. When playing on the G-string, your left elbow should be tucked under the violin so that your fingers get directed towards the G-string, and the elbow level of your bow hand will be higher than usual.

The exercise below is also a great exercise in bowing technique. Try to play each quarter note with a whole bow starting at the heel of the bow. Then, play each eighth note with a half bow alternating at the upper and lower half of the bow. Play slowly to get the bow distribution right. If you are having trouble reaching D with your fourth finger, bring your elbow even further under the violin and soften your thumb.

WB – Whole Bow
UH – Upper Half
LH – Lower Half

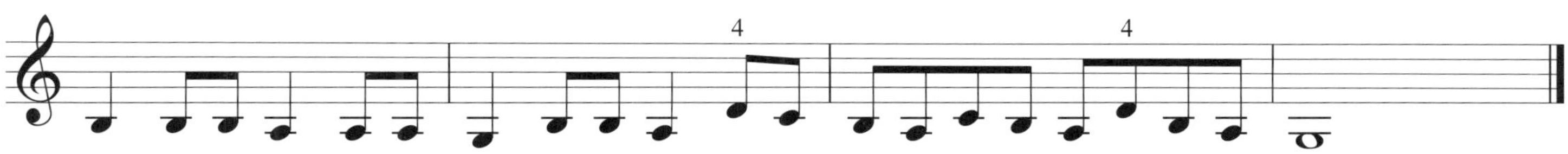

Practicing Funeral March

TOOLBOX

Sixteenth Notes

Sixteenth notes are played twice as fast as eighth notes. You can subdivide the beat by using a 4-syllable word such as "pea-nut but-ter." On a single note, try alternating between quarter notes, eighth notes, and sixteenth notes. Focus on keeping a steady beat and even note lengths.

Eighth notes and sixteenth notes are often beamed together. In "Funeral March," we see a dotted eighth note plus a sixteenth note. Break down the dotted eighth note into four sixteenth notes, and you know exactly how fast to play the one sixteenth note.

In "Funeral March," we alternate playing two notes up bow and two notes down bow with the same bow direction. These notes are not slurred notes as we know them; we cannot slur two notes that are the same pitch, as you would not hear the individual notes. In this case, we stop the bow very briefly between the two notes, so you hear a slight separation. The dash below the eighth note is called a *tenuto* and indicates to play these notes with the same bow direction, but make them sound as if they are separate bows.

FUNERAL MARCH

from PIANO SONATA IN B-FLAT MINOR, OP. 35

By Fryderyk Chopin

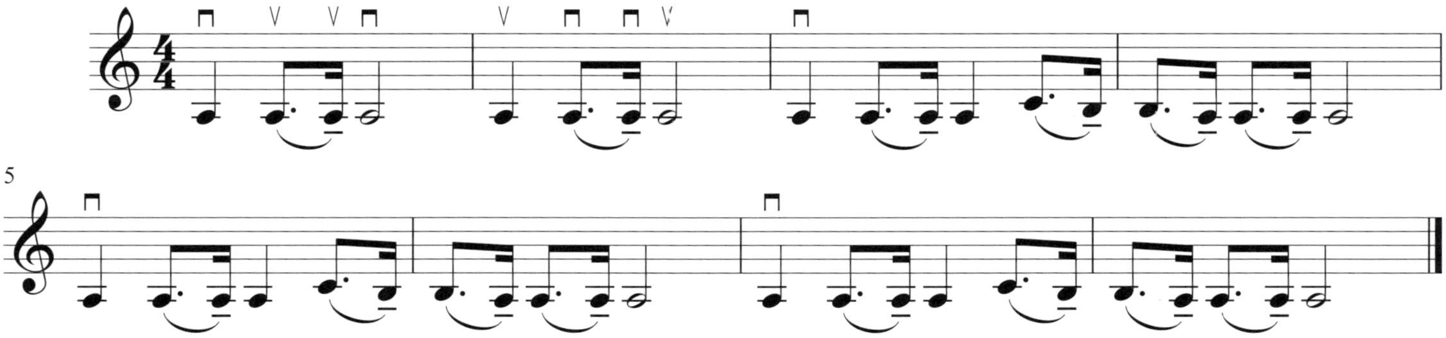

Notes on the E-String

In the next exercise, count 4 beats for each note and aim to play with a straight bow. Drop your right shoulder and upper arm to play the correct string level when playing on the E-string.

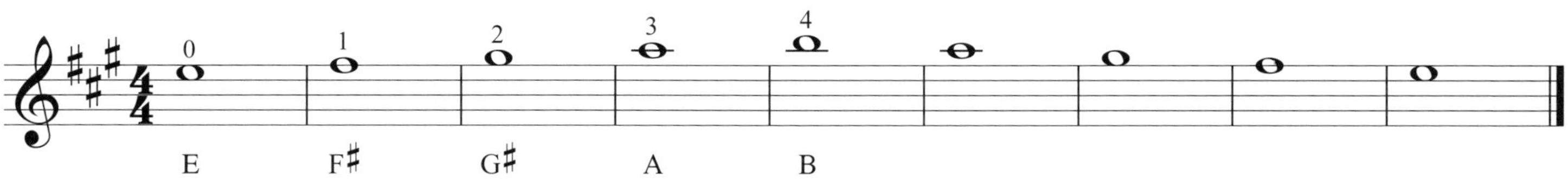

TOOLBOX

Triplets

A *triplet* is when a beat is divided into three equal notes and are written twice as fast as the note it represents. An eighth note triplet fits in the space of one quarter note. Quarter note triplets are played in the time of one half note. Play triplets very lazily with a zigzag bowing across a whole bow.

CAN'T HELP FALLING IN LOVE

Words and Music by George David Weiss, Hugo Peretti and Luigi Creatore

LESSON 7:
Double Stops

Up to this point, we've been practicing playing individual notes. *Double stops* is a technique where you deliberately play more than one note. Pieces sometimes have one or more double stops to produce a bigger sound. We can play two notes at the same time on the violin because of the way the bridge is shaped. Occasionally, violinists will play three notes together, a technique called *playing chords*, which we will look at in Lesson 21.

When we play two strings at the same time, it is our right elbow that determines the string level of the bow. Let's begin by playing the open strings two-by-two.

Using Double Stops to Improve Intonation

Double stops can be used to help us improve our intonation and to check our tuning during pieces. The third finger on the D-, A-, and E-string will have the same letter name as the string below. Play the exercises below slowly, listening carefully to the tuning of each note. When you play double stops, try to blend your notes perfectly together. You have three measures to adjust your third finger to achieve perfect tuning.

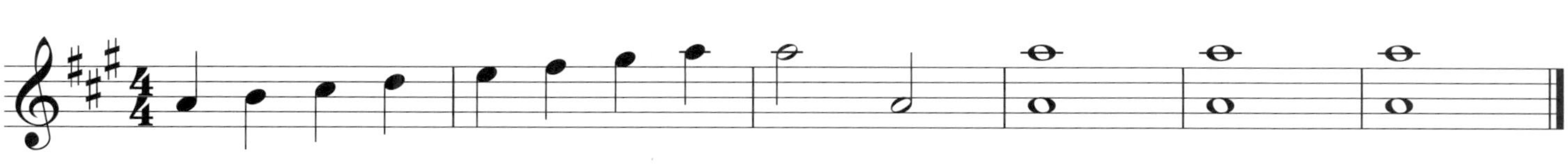

When playing double stops, violinists tend to read the lower note first, followed by the top note. This skill is particularly valuable when we play chords, so let's get into the habit of reading double stops from the bottom up right away.

Any two notes on adjacent strings can be played as double stops, as you will find in "Amazing Grace." Watch the video for tips on how to develop your bowing for double stops.

We will be playing in 3/4 time. Use a whole bow for each note or slur. You will find that each down bow will move at half the pace of each up bow. Be careful not to play too strongly on the up bows, as the main emphasis should always be played on the first beat of the bar. Bow extremely slowly on the tied notes in bars 7-8 and 15-16.

AMAZING GRACE

Words by John Newton
Traditional American Melody

LESSON 8:
Playing with Expression

To make musical performances more expressive and therefore more convincing to listen to, composers add performance directions to the music. Many performance directions are in Italian. *Dynamics* tell us how loud or soft to play.

Dynamics from Loud to Soft:

ff	*fortissimo*	very loud
f	*forte*	loud
mf	*mezzo forte*	medium loud
mp	*mezzo piano*	medium soft
p	*piano*	soft
pp	*pianissimo*	very soft

The volume of your playing is determined by three factors:

1) **The amount of bow you're using.** More bow = louder, less bow = softer.

2) **The contact point of the bow on the string.** Closer to the bridge = louder, closer to the fingerboard = softer.

3) **The weight of the bow on the string.** More weight = louder, less weight = softer.

Changes in Volume

To change between dynamics, you need to use more or less bow, change the position of the bow on the string, and add or remove weight from the bow on the string. *Crescendo* (*cresc.*) means to gradually become louder and *decrescendo* (*decresc.*) means to gradually become softer. Changes in volume can also be indicated by lines (often referred to by musicians as *hairpins*) such as the ones below.

gradually getting louder → gradually getting softer

p < ***f*** > ***p***

crescendo (*cresc.*) decrescendo (*decresc.*)

In "Hey Jude," make the contrast between the soft and loud sections as prominent as you can by adjusting your bow length and the contact point of the bow on the string.

Watch the video for additional instruction on bowing and fingering.

HEY JUDE

Demo/Backing

Words and Music by John Lennon and Paul McCartney

Practicing Largo

Look at "Largo" from the *New World Symphony*. Can you find where the changes in loudness are indicated in the music? Start softly, then as the music develops, play a little louder. You will find that in this piece the dynamic levels are subtle. Bear in mind that all dynamic markings are relative. How soft is soft depends on your instrument, the style of the music, what you want to express in your music, and what other dynamics are in the piece.

"Largo" is a legato piece. You will see lots of slurs, and if you already know the tune, you will know that the melody is played smoothly with no abrupt bowings, movements, or sounds.

The word *largo* means slow. How slow exactly you will play this piece is up to you. It depends on what mood you want to evoke with the piece. However, there is a certain tradition of how this piece is usually performed, and at a beginner level, you may stick to the traditional way of playing this. It is useful to listen to various performances as you learn to play this piece. At the end of the music, we have two new music markings.

TOOLBOX

Ritardando and Rallentando

Ritardando (*rit.*) and *rallentando* (*rall.*) mean to gradually get slower.

TOOLBOX

Fermata

A *fermata* indicates to hold a note longer than its original value. If you are playing with a group, watch the conductor or leader to know when to continue playing.

Try to use the fourth finger wherever indicated in the music. As the music is slow and flowing in style, we want to avoid crossing strings wherever possible so that our bowing is calm and even, especially during slurs.

LARGO

from SYMPHONY NO. 9 IN E MINOR, OP. 95
("FROM THE NEW WORLD")

By Antonin Dvorak

VIOLIN TALK

You will notice that as you become a more advanced player, there will be more information in the music. You will gradually become familiar with more musical terms, so take it slowly at this stage and take in one thing at a time.

LESSON 9:
Key Signatures

In previous lessons, we learned to play scales and arpeggios. In this chapter, we will look in greater detail at what these keys mean and why it is useful to understand musical keys.

The foundation of Western classical music is the scale. You may have learned to sing a scale: do, re, mi, fa, sol, la, ti, do when you were younger. The C major scale, often used in piano music, is made up of the following notes: C-D-EF-G-A-BC. We will learn to play the C major scale later, but for now, we will use it to help us understand how a scale is constructed.

As you know, notes are named with the letters of the alphabet. Every two letters of the alphabet are a *whole tone* apart, except for B-C and E-F. These two intervals are a *semitone* or *half step*. Note that in the C major scale above, the letters EF and BC are written close together, indicating the semitones.

Think back to when we were learning to place our fingers on the fingerboard. There were times when there was space between our fingers and times when we placed one finger directly beside the other. **When playing whole tones, there is a space between your fingers. When playing semitones, there is no space between your fingers.**

Major scales that start on different notes sound the same because they follow a specific pattern of whole tones and semitones between each of the notes.

C	D	E	F	G	A	B	C
Tone	Tone	Semitone	Tone	Tone	Tone	Semitone	

We know already that a sharp (♯) raises a note by a semitone. So, if we wanted to play a D major scale, to keep the same pattern of notes we would add two sharps: C♯ and F♯.

D	E	F♯	G	A	B	C♯	D
Tone	Tone	Semitone	Tone	Tone	Tone	Semitone	

Next, let's check out the pattern of the A major scale:

A	B	C♯	D	E	F♯	G♯	A
Tone	Tone	Semitone	Tone	Tone	Tone	Semitone	

If we want to keep the same pattern of tones and semitones, the A major scale will need three sharps: F♯, C♯, and G♯.

TOOLBOX

Review: Key Signatures and Accidentals

A *key signature* at the beginning of our music indicates which notes to play sharp or flat. The line or space that the sharp or flat occupies indicates which notes are changed. They are based on scales and the accidentals will always appear in the same order.

G Major D Major A Major E Major

An *accidental* is a sharp (♯), flat (♭), or natural sign (♮) that appears in music. Accidentals override whatever is marked in the key signature and are good for an entire measure. A *natural* sign (♮) will "cancel" a sharp or flat.

Sliding Fingers

Let's now think about how to play the D♯, which is played by raising the third finger on the A-string. Slide your third finger from the D to the D♯. Try not to hop your finger from one note to the next. Instead, slide your fingertip along the string. Aim to sync the timing of your slide with the bowing. Remember the bar line cancels an accidental so the third note is a D♮. Lower your finger back to D before you move your finger up to D♯ again.

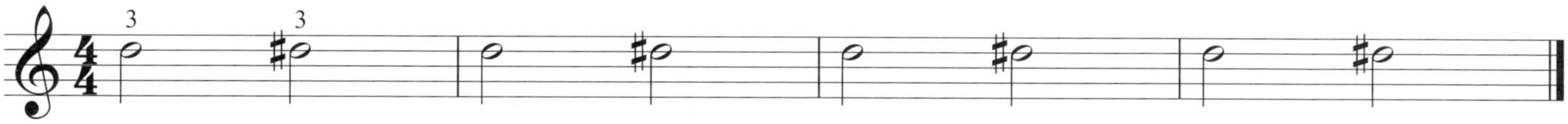

Let's practice the same technique on the D-string, sliding your third finger from G to G♯ and back. Note that the way we write the sharp is in front of the note, "sharp G," but we say "G sharp."

Now let's practice sliding down to the C using the second finger. Note the natural sign (♮) on the second C which cancels the sharp. C natural is lower pitched than C♯.

Let's also practice sliding the second finger on the D-string. Note the F♯ in the key signature. While this F♯ is on the top staff line, the sharp sign affects all Fs in the music; high or low, it does not matter.

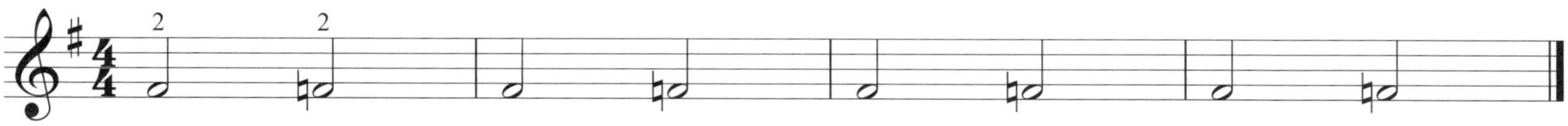

Practicing 10,000 Reasons (Bless the Lord)

"10,000 Reasons (Bless the Lord)" is written in the key of G major. You will have noticed one sharp in the key signature, F♯. This means that the second finger on the D-string is sharp. You have always played this finger in this position.

However, the second finger on the A-string is now a C (in the past we always played C♯). This finger is placed next to the first finger on A. You remember that the interval B-C was a semitone. When playing semitones, there is no space between your fingers.

Other things of note:

- There are quite a few dynamic markings in this piece. Try to make them as expressive as you can.
- Start in the middle of the bow so you can use a whole bow on the quarter note E.
- In bar 10, place one finger on both the E- and A-string.
- In bar 18, to play the C natural, place your second finger right beside your first finger.
- This is the longest piece we've played so far. Build your stamina by playing through the entire piece without stopping.

TOOLBOX

Multi-Measure Rests

When you have multiple measures of rests in a row, we combine those rests into one bar; the number on the top indicates how many bars of rest to count.

In "10,000 Reasons," if you play along with the original recording, there are three bars of rest before the vocal comes in on beat 4 of the fourth bar.

10,000 REASONS (BLESS THE LORD)

Words and Music by Jonas Myrin and Matt Redman

VIOLIN TALK

Make a habit of always practicing each new piece slowly. This will give you time to work out the details of the notes and rhythms and allow you to play with as few mistakes as possible. Each time you repeat a mistake, you get better at it, so it's a good idea to try to avoid mistakes in the first place by playing very slowly.

Before you begin any piece, look at the time signature and key signature. You can add performance directions once you have learned the notes and rhythms.

LESSON 10:
The C Major Scale

The C major scale has no sharps or flats in its key signature. This means that we will play natural notes throughout. We will also use this scale to improve our intonation.

When the second finger on the D- and A-strings are placed immediately beside the first finger, they are called F♮ and C♮. You may remember from Lesson 9 that the intervals E-F and B-C are semitones, and we play semitones with our fingers close together.

The first finger on the E-string is called F♮. The finger sits right at the beginning of the E-string. Now, when you play G♮, the second finger on the E-string, this note is a space away from the first finger (a low second finger), because F-G are a tone apart. Play A with your third finger by placing it a space apart from your second finger (G). Add another space with your fourth finger to play B.

Now to our top note, the high C. This note is a semitone (half step) away from the fourth finger B. We can play the top C with a stretched fourth finger—it's very close to the B. After playing the B, slide your fourth finger up to the C. If you find it challenging to reach the stretched fourth finger, try softening your left thumb and getting it upright. Let's compare the fingering pattern we've learned previously with the pattern for the C major scale.

Normal:

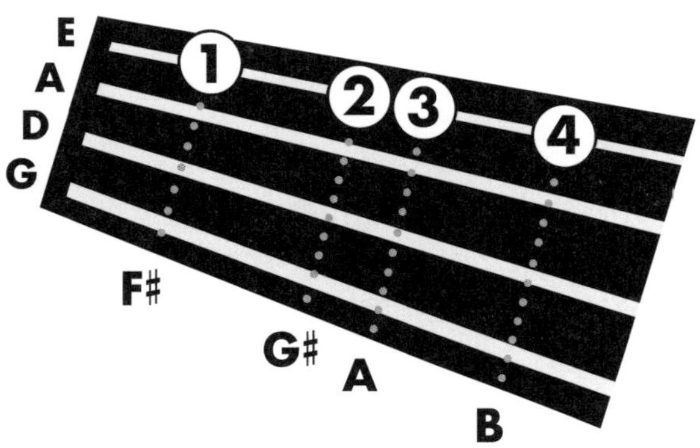

C Major:

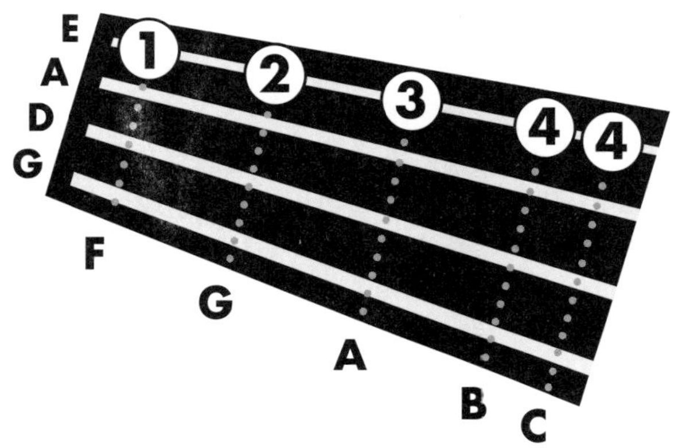

Notice that there is a double stop in three places. Here you can check your tuning with the open string.

VIOLIN TALK

Position Check

Before you play, check the position of your left thumb and left wrist. Your thumb should be upright and just peeking over the fingerboard. Your wrist should be straight but not stiff and free from the neck and body of the violin.

Practicing Fly Me to the Moon (In Other Words)

"Fly Me to the Moon" is written in the key of C major, so there are no sharps or flats in the key signature. There are a couple of accidentals—notes that are not part of the key signature—causing a raised third finger on the G- and D-strings (C♯ and G♯). Remember that accidentals last until the next bar line. In bar 59, the ♯ for the first G♯ also affects the second G.

When you listen to songs that were originally written for voice such as "Fly Me to the Moon," you sometimes hear tricky rhythms or glissandi (sliding notes) not notated in the music. Unlike in classical music where violinists are expected to play precisely what is written, in popular music this aspect of musicianship is much more free. Listen to different recordings and experiment with adding your own inflections to the music.

Other things of note:

- Count the first four bars and subsequent 16 bars of rest carefully. On the audio, the piano enters on beat 2. There will be 9 "clicks" at the start of the audio to help count you in.
- Use a raised third finger for C♯ and G♯.
- Experiment playing D with the fourth finger and open string. Use whichever is most comfortable.
- Bars 26 and 58, use a fourth finger A to make finding the G♯ easier.

TOOLBOX

Swing Eighths

Swing eighths is a type of rhythmic feel. In a pair of eighth notes, the first note will last a little bit longer than the second. So, in a set of four eighth notes, it will sound, "long-short-long-short." However, to make reading the notes easier, the eighth notes are printed as even notes. This concept is best learned by listening.

FLY ME TO THE MOON (IN OTHER WORDS)

Demo/Backing

Words and Music by Bart Howard

LESSON 11:
Playing Flats

Just like we can raise notes by adding sharps to them, we can lower notes by adding flats (♭). A flat in front of a note lowers the note by a semitone. When you play flats on your violin, lower your finger on the string. As with sharps, we call a note "B-flat," but in your music, the accidental is written before the note.

Let's practice the B♭ on the A-string. Make sure that you slide your finger instead of hopping. Your fingertip should stay in contact with the string, albeit lightly, when you slide.

This brings us to a weird inconsistency in the note names on the violin. Let's practice lowering the first finger on the E-string.

While this, is in essence, the same exercise as the B-B♭ exercise, the notes are called F♯ for the "normal" first finger on the E-string, and F♮ for the low first finger. This is just something that you'll have to learn. There is no consistency or pattern to it, sadly.

Like the sharps, flats also always appear in the same order on the staff when used in a key signature. From left to right, the flats are called B♭, E♭, A♭, and D♭.

Playing E-Flat

Let's think about the E♭ next. The E♭ is an E which has been made lower. Therefore, we cannot play the E♭ on the E-string. Instead, you will play the E♭ with the fourth finger on the A-string. The E♭ is located beside the D, which is the third finger on the A-string.

Check out the exercise below. We are playing the fingers on the A-string first, so we can find the E♭ next to the third finger. Note that when you play the first bar, there is a C♯, so there is a space between your first and second finger. When you play C♯, D, and E♭ (fingers 2, 3, and 4), all your fingers are close together. Play very slowly and try to leave the third finger down, even when you play the open E-string. The dotted line indicates this. At first, you may find this very challenging, but this should become easier with practice. Bring your left elbow further under the violin to create a "tunnel" under your fingers so that the E-string can ring freely. It may take a few days before you'll manage this. Take your time; it is a good technique to learn.

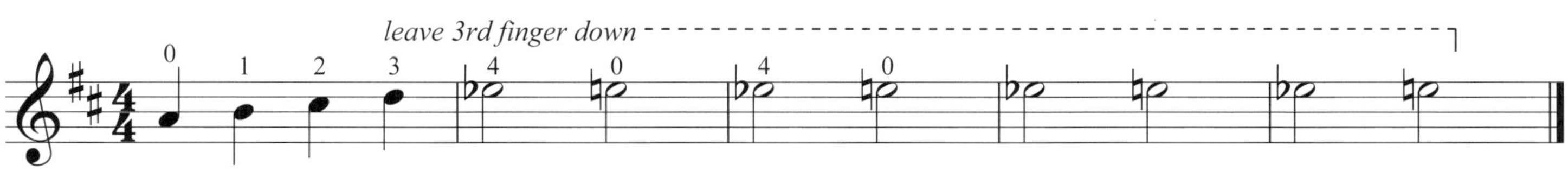

Practicing Edelweiss

In "Edelweiss," we have two flats in the key signature, B♭ and E♭. Unlike our previous exercise, the E♭ played with the fourth finger on the A-string does not appear here. Instead, we come across the low E♭, which is played by pulling the first finger on the D-string back to the beginning of the string. The same happens when you play the B♭, which is a low first finger on the A-string.

Think about the second fingers now. To play F, the second finger on the D-string, we use a low second finger. Because our first finger is already low for the E♭, there is a gap between fingers one and two. The same is true for the A-string when playing B♭-C. You may find this mind-boggling initially. Many players do. Take your time to learn this challenging piece. You are making progress and that's the main thing.

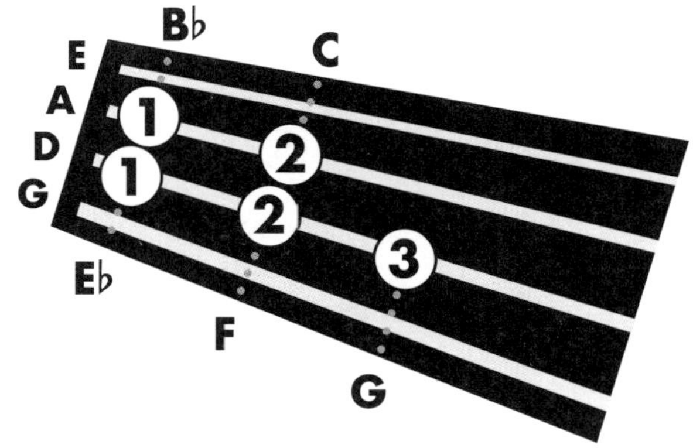

Have you noticed that we have not really thought about the bow distribution for a while? That has become second nature now. That's awesome progress!

EDELWEISS

Demo/Backing

from THE SOUND OF MUSIC

Lyrics by Oscar Hammerstein II

Music by Richard Rodgers

LESSON 12:
Martelé Bowing

In Lesson 8, we learned how to play louds and softs. In this chapter, we will be learning two new performance directions, *staccato* and *accents*.

Staccato

Staccato (short) is the opposite of *legato* (smooth) which we came across earlier. Music notes with dots above them indicate that they are to be played staccato. While staccato is the name of the sound, the bowing technique that we will use to play staccato is called *martelé*. Martelé in French means hammered, and this bow stroke generates a percussive sound. In martelé bowing, we make use of the natural springiness of the bow.

Martelé is produced by holding the bow against the string with pressure, then releasing it explosively to produce a sharp, biting sound with a rest between bow strokes. Squeeze your bow hand at the beginning and end of each bow stroke and play at the upper half of the bow.

In "Friend Like Me," we are playing with two flats in our key signature. Before adding martelé bowing to the music, practice the notes and rhythms.

Other things of note:

- Use your fourth finger to play E♭ on the A-string, and high B♭ on the E-string.
- All Cs in the piece are sharp; place your second finger on the A-string in its normal position.
- Use a low second finger on the E-string to play G.
- The G♯ in bar 15 lies immediately below the third finger.

TOOLBOX

Accents

When you see the accent (>) in the music, play this note more strongly.

FRIEND LIKE ME

Demo/Backing

from ALADDIN

Music by Alan Menken
Lyrics by Howard Ashman

LESSON 13:
The Chromatic Scale

Now that you can change your finger positions, you can learn to play a *chromatic scale*. The word *chromatic* comes from the Greek word *chromos*, which means color. In a chromatic scale, every note is a semitone away from one another. Try to memorize the fingering when you play the chromatic scale. It is an often-used pattern that you will come across in many pieces in the future.

Notice that the note we called E♭ in "Friend Like Me" is now called D♯. These notes sound the same and we play these with the same finger, but they are named differently. The E♭ is a variant of E, and the D♯ is a variant of D. We call these notes *enharmonic equivalents*.

When you play chromatic scales, try to leave your fingers on the string, and slide—rather than hop—from one note to the next. There should be no gaps in the sound.

Polishing Exercise – Watch this video for further practice exercises on sliding your finger between notes.

Chromatic Scale Practice

Chromatic Scale Starting on A:

Chromatic Scale Starting on D:

Chromatic Scale Starting on G:

Now for a challenge: Can you play a chromatic scale with a dotted rhythm? The fingering is the same as before. Aim to synchronize your left and right hands perfectly.

Milestone 3

You have developed your left hand so that it can play any note on each of the strings. Well done!

LESSON 14:
More Bowing Technique

Let's review the types of bowing techniques we've learned so far.

Legato Bow Strokes:

- Detaché: Detached notes, alternating between down bow and up bow, as we have practiced in the early sections of this book. The word detaché is slightly misleading; the bow strokes are separate, as opposed to slurred, but there are no gaps—no silences—between the notes.
- Slurred notes: Two or more notes played on one bow.

Staccato Bow Strokes:

- Martelé: played at the upper half of the bow. The staccato effect is created by squeezing and releasing the bow.

Spiccato

Spiccato is another type of staccato bowing technique and is a jumping or hopping bow stroke at the balance point of the bow. Spiccato bowing has three main characteristics:

1. It is played at the balance point of the bow.
2. The right elbow gives the impulse.
3. The fingers of the right hand act as shock absorbers.

Let's find the balance point of the bow. The balance point of the bow varies from one bow to the next. Try resting the bow on one finger and find the exact spot where your bow is perfectly balanced. It is probably somewhere around here:

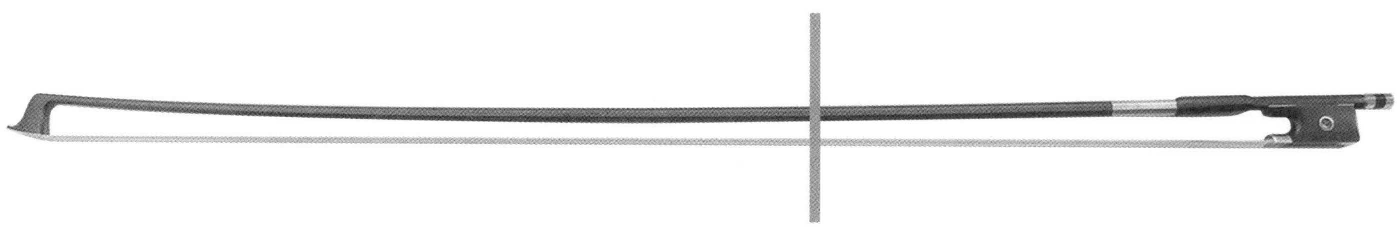

Once you have found the balance point, you can mark it with a pencil line or sticker, so that you can find it easily when you play.

When you practice the following exercise, try to leave your right shoulder in its lowest position, and soften your bow-hand fingers.

In "Dance of the Sugar Plum Fairy," make sure you are playing at the balance point of the bow. Re-take and start with a down bow every four bars. It will make that bar much easier to play. Also, re-take the bow at the start of bar 3 and similar bars. Playing two up bows in the last bar will make the E-string ring beautifully and is an added bit of fun at the end.

DANCE OF THE SUGAR PLUM FAIRY

from THE NUTCRACKER SUITE, OP. 71A

By Pyotr Il'yich Tchaikovsky

Practicing Minuet No. 2 in G Major

In this Minuet—an elegant, stately dance—legato and staccato bars alternate. This gives the piece its lively character. Note the up bow staccato in the second bar. Use a martelé bow stroke for these notes. The two up bows help you to move towards the middle of the bow and prepare you for the detaché notes in the second bar.

Other things of note:

- Start legato at the upper half of the bow and leave the bow on the string.
- Bar 2 beat 1, play through to the point of the bow, and use martelé bowing at the tip of the bow for the staccato notes.
- Bar 15, the eighth note triplet should fit evenly into one beat. In the last two beats, shoot off the second staccato so you end at the heel of the bow and can use a whole bow in bar 16.
- Bar 17, to play softly, play in the middle of the bow. Use short bows and move the bow away from the bridge toward the fingerboard.
- Bar 24, to play the crescendo, increase the length of the bow used. Steer the bow towards the bridge and press harder.
- Make a noticeable contrast between the loud and soft sections.

As always, play very slowly, particularly when you first learn this piece.

MINUET NO. 2 IN G MAJOR

By Johann Sebastian Bach

LESSON 15:
Simple and Compound Time

You already know about 3/4 and 4/4 time, where you count 3 and 4 beats in a bar respectively. These time signatures are also known as *simple time*, where each beat can be divided into two. You count these "1-and 2-and 3-and 4-and."

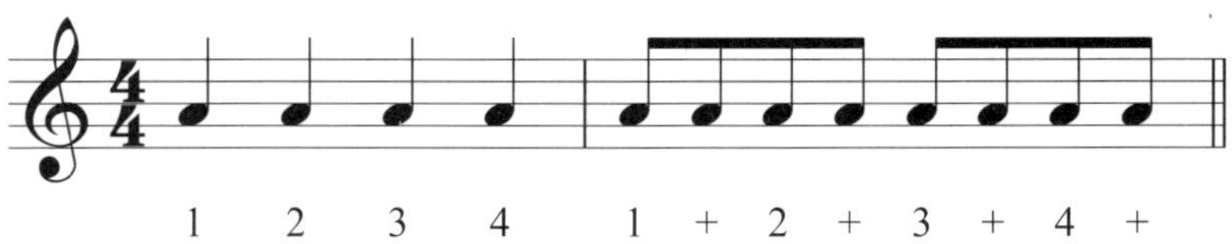

In this lesson, we will learn a new time signature, 6/8 time. In each bar, there are six eighth notes. The six beats are organized into two groups of three. Let's practice counting with the following exercise.

Time signatures such as 6/8 time are called *compound time*. In compound time, each beat is divided into three parts. The first beat in the bar is always the strongest. Emphasizing the first beat in the bar while you play will give your music a nice lilt.

You can practice this lilt in "The Irish Washerwoman." Notice how when you play in 6/8 time you might count this in two, **1**23 **4**56. Your strongest accent falls on 1, and there is a secondary accent on 4.

The key signature has one sharp, F♯. C on the A-string and G on the E-string are natural, so use a low second finger.

TOOLBOX

1st and 2nd Endings

Play through the 1st ending like a standard repeat sign and return to the forward repeat sign. On the second time through, skip the 1st ending and play the 2nd ending.

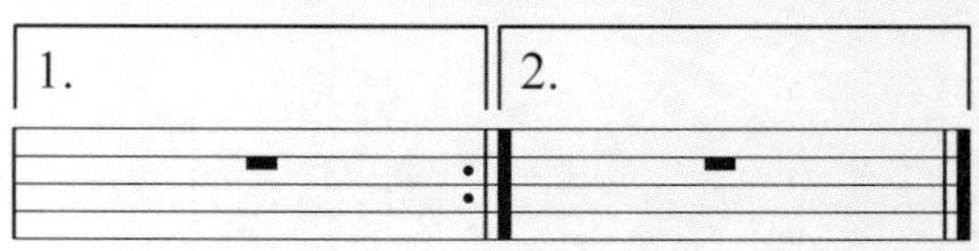

THE IRISH WASHERWOMAN

Irish Folksong

VIOLIN TALK

Now that you are making such good progress, please keep playing slowly. Slow practice will allow you to play faster in the long term. There is a saying in violin playing that goes "Slow is Fast" and it is categorically true.

So far, we have learned pieces with the same time signature throughout the piece. Some composers, however, combine different time signatures into one piece. An example is "America" from *West Side Story*.

Watch the video for tips on improving your intonation in bars 11 and 12.

AMERICA Demo/Backing

from WEST SIDE STORY

Lyrics by Stephen Sondheim
Music by Leonard Bernstein

Practicing Hallelujah

In "Hallelujah," we are playing in 6/8 time and in the key of C major. Use very short bows for the sixteenth notes and stress the first beat in each bar. You will have noticed that the crescendos and decrescendos are very long and drawn out. Make these as gradual as you possibly can. When you play the very last note, let your bow move very slowly, close to the fingerboard, so that the music dies down completely.

Watch the video for additional arm exercises to aid in the relaxation of the right arm and shoulder.

HALLELUJAH Demo/Backing

Words and Music by Leonard Cohen

82
2
mf
88
93
98
103
108
4
2
mf
114
119
124
f
129
134
27

Practicing Take Five

The time signature in "Take Five" is 5/4 time. This means that there are five quarter notes in each bar. So, we count **12345 12345**, with the emphasis on 1. However, the melody has a pickup so you start on beat 4.

This is a jazz song, so the eighth notes are played swung, the same as when we played "Fly Me to the Moon."

In the second bar of the violin part, there is an A#. This note is played with the first finger. Remember, an accidental lasts until the bar line, so the third note is also an A#. You have played this note in earlier pieces as a B♭. Since we have the second finger available, you can use that to play the B, rather than shifting the first finger up. This will feel a bit odd at first, but we want to avoid playing the same finger on three notes in a row. Pay close attention also to the marked fingerings in bars 14 and 15.

You may notice the two up bow staccato notes in bar 5. Two up bows in a row help us to move towards the heel of the bow and prepare for the long down bow E that follows.

This is another big piece for you to learn, so give yourself time to familiarize yourself with the music and play slowly. It may well take some players a couple of weeks to learn, and that is totally normal.

TAKE FIVE Demo/Backing

By Paul Desmond

Milestone 4

You can recognize key signatures and time signatures in music, and you know their meaning. You can play with expression in your musical performance. You can play jazzy pieces as well as popular classics. Congratulations! That's awesome progress.

LESSON 16:
Building Stamina

You will have noticed that both "Fly Me to the Moon" and "Hallelujah" required considerably more stamina as your pieces have gradually become longer. Take regular breaks if your shoulders, arms, or hands get tired. Review your bow hold and violin hold (Lesson 2) from time to time. In this chapter, we will play some pieces in different keys to help you develop toward being able to take on new material independently. You will also notice that within a piece of music, the key signature may change.

In "Colors of the Wind," we are playing in 4/4 time. The key signature at the start is one flat. While the B♭ does not appear in your violin part, it does in the accompaniment. Note that in bar 11, the key signature changes to two sharps, so from that moment on, your second fingers will need to get higher on the D- and A-strings.

Bring out the louds and softs in the music. You will notice in vocal music in sections where the notes are higher pitched, the music is often louder.

COLORS OF THE WIND

Demo/Backing

from POCAHONTAS

Music by Alan Menken

Lyrics by Stephen Schwartz

rit.
a tempo
rit.
a tempo
rit.

In "In the Hall of the Mountain King," we come across several new techniques. In bar 6, there is an E♯. Play this note with a raised first finger. E♯ is the same note as F and a half step below F♯, which you played at the end of bar 5. Therefore, your first finger sits immediately next to the second finger.

In bar 13, there is an A♯. The first time this A♯ appears we will play it with a fourth finger on the D-string. As this is a rather large stretch for your fourth finger, imagine you "walk up" your fingers through the raised third finger. Releasing any tension in your left thumb will enable your pinky to reach for the fourth finger too. This way it will flow nicely with the notes on the D-string. Towards the end of bar 13, there is another A♯ which we will play with the first finger on the A-string. As we now have the first finger on the A♯, the C♯ is played by the third finger and the D by the fourth finger. This is called *playing in the half position* as we now have all our fingers a half step further back. Being able to play in the half position is a very useful skill. Play extremely slowly while you are getting used to the different fingers playing different notes. Many players find playing in the half position quite confusing, so it is okay to take your time to learn this technique.

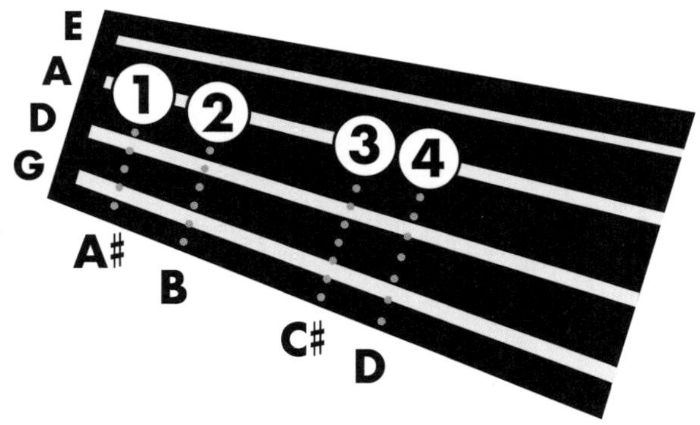

Practice playing "In the Hall of the Mountain King" with the bow on the string first. Play slowly and make sure that all the notes are in tune before playing faster. Eventually, you may want to play the whole piece spiccato.

TOOLBOX

Dynamic Changes During Repeats

Dynamic markings with a hyphen mean that the first time through the music you play the first dynamic, and on the repeat, you play the second dynamic.

mp-mf

TOOLBOX

Accelerando

Accelerando (*accel.*) means to gradually get faster.

IN THE HALL OF THE MOUNTAIN KING

from PEER GYNT

By Edvard Grieg

LESSON 17:
The Third Position

Now that you are accomplished in playing in different keys, it is time to expand your range of notes and learn to play in the third position. Positions on the violin are like frets on a guitar. As we move our left hand up and along the fingerboard, we can play higher notes on each string.

It may be clear why we want to play higher notes on the E-string, some pieces contain notes that are higher than the top C that we have learned up until now. However, when we play higher notes on the G-, D-, and A-strings, we can vary the timbre of notes compared with when we play those same notes on a higher string. Playing in third position can thus also be used as a means of expression.

Third Position Notes on the A-String

When you play in the third position, your first finger will be where you normally place your third finger. When you move to this position, make sure that your left thumb comes up to the third position too. Your thumb should still be opposite your index finger. There will be a space between fingers one and two, and two and three. Fingers three and four are together. So, 1-2-34.

In the exercise below, compare the spacing between the first and third positions.

First Position:	**Third Position:**
1-23-4	1-2-34

Testing notes for intonation is vital for playing in tune in the third position. When you are learning, test your fingers with open strings whenever you can.

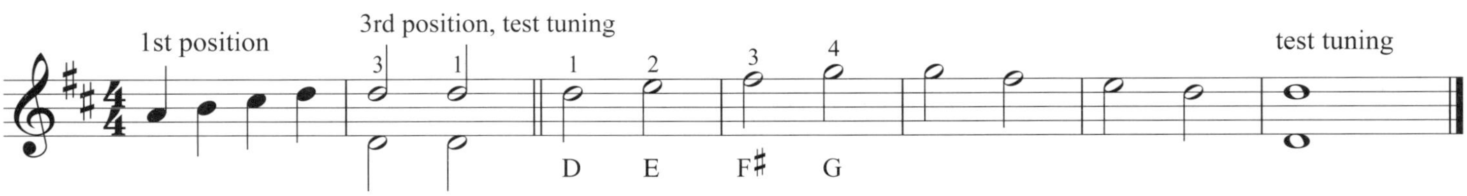

The first three bars in "Super Trouper" show you how to find your starting note. Take your time to find your fingers. When you begin to play, go slowly, and listen very carefully to the tuning of each note. Note that there are two sharps in the key signature, so there is a whole tone between the E played by the second finger, and the F♯ played by the third finger. Therefore, your third position finger pattern is 1-2-34. The third and fourth fingers are F♯ and G.

In bar 5, place your third finger along with your fourth finger at the same time.

SUPER TROUPER

Words and Music by Benny Andersson and Björn Ulvaeus

Third Position Notes on the E-String

As we did with the A-string notes, check your tuning with the open string. Once it is good, swap your third finger for your first finger and check your tuning again. Double-check that your thumb is aligned with your first finger and just peeking over the edge. The spacing of the fingers on the E-string in the third position will be the same as the A-string 1-2-34.

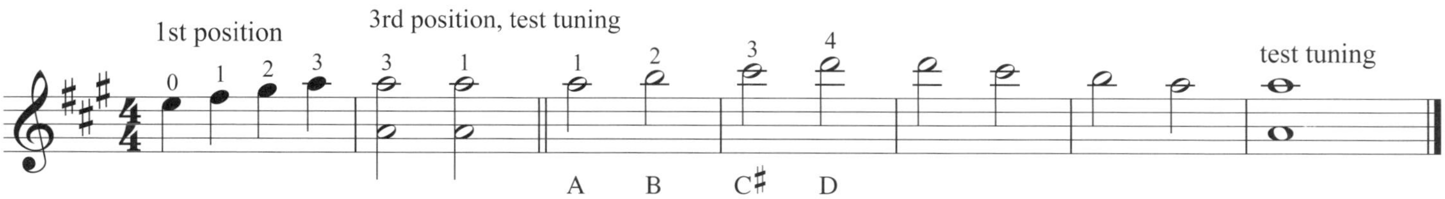

EVERY BREATH YOU TAKE

Music and Lyrics by Sting

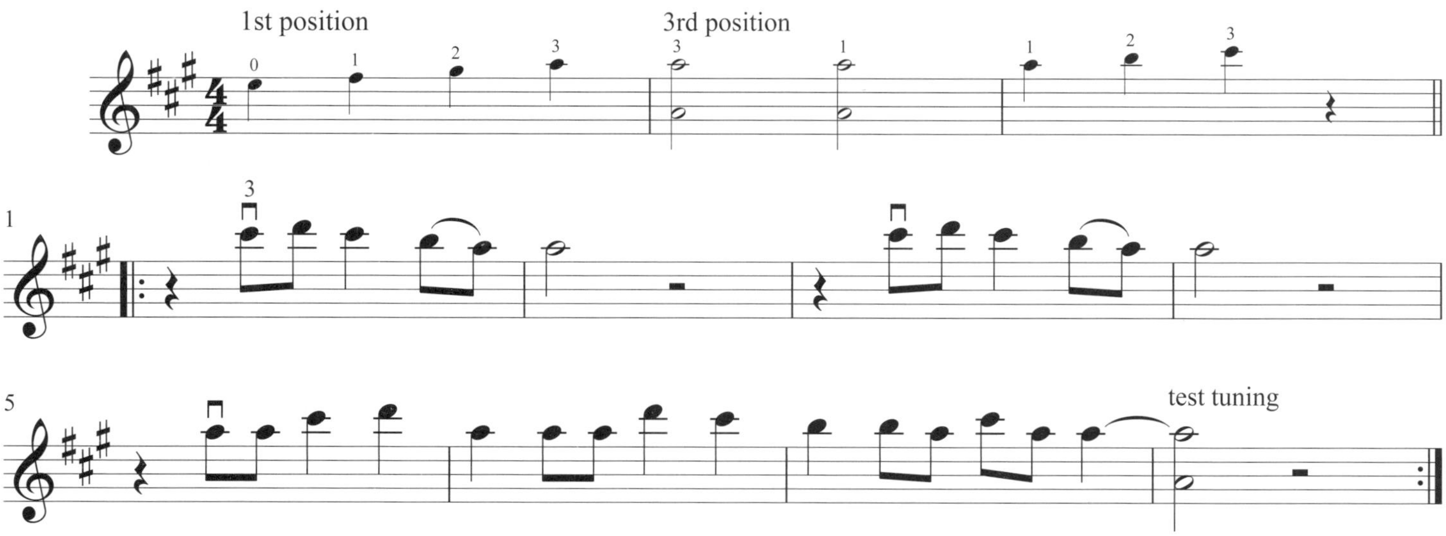

Third Position Notes on the D-String

Note the key signature and your finger pattern when playing the notes on the D-string. When you test your fingers, there is an F♯. When you play bars 3 and 4, the finger pattern is 1-2-34. Remember B-C is a half step. Be sure to tuck your elbow as far under the violin as possible.

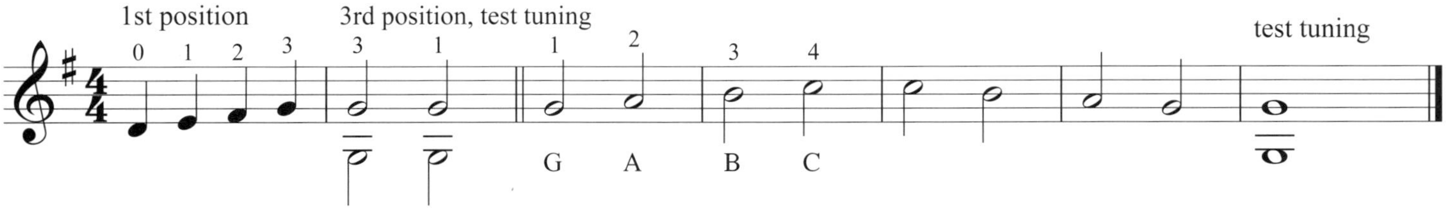

In "Bad Romance," not only can you check the tuning of the first finger with the open G-string, but you can also check the tuning of the second finger with the open A-string (bar 3). That's why the note has two stems: one for the open A and one for the A with the second finger. You will find that when you test your fingers frequently in the early stages of your learning, you will gradually begin to "feel" where the third position is.

BAD ROMANCE

Words and Music by Stefani Germanotta and Nadir Khayat

Third Position Notes on the G-String

When you play in the third position on the G-string, you will find that you will need to bring your left elbow further under the violin to be able to reach the G-string with all your fingers. Take a look at the key signature here: no sharps or flats. Once again, in the third position we use the finger pattern 1-2-34.

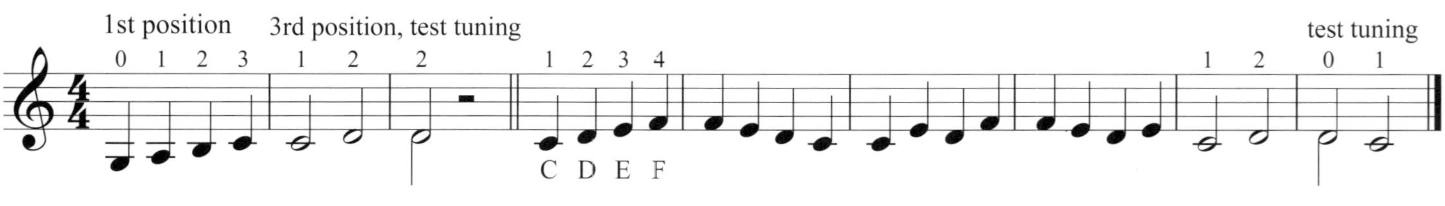

LEAN ON ME

Words and Music by Bill Withers

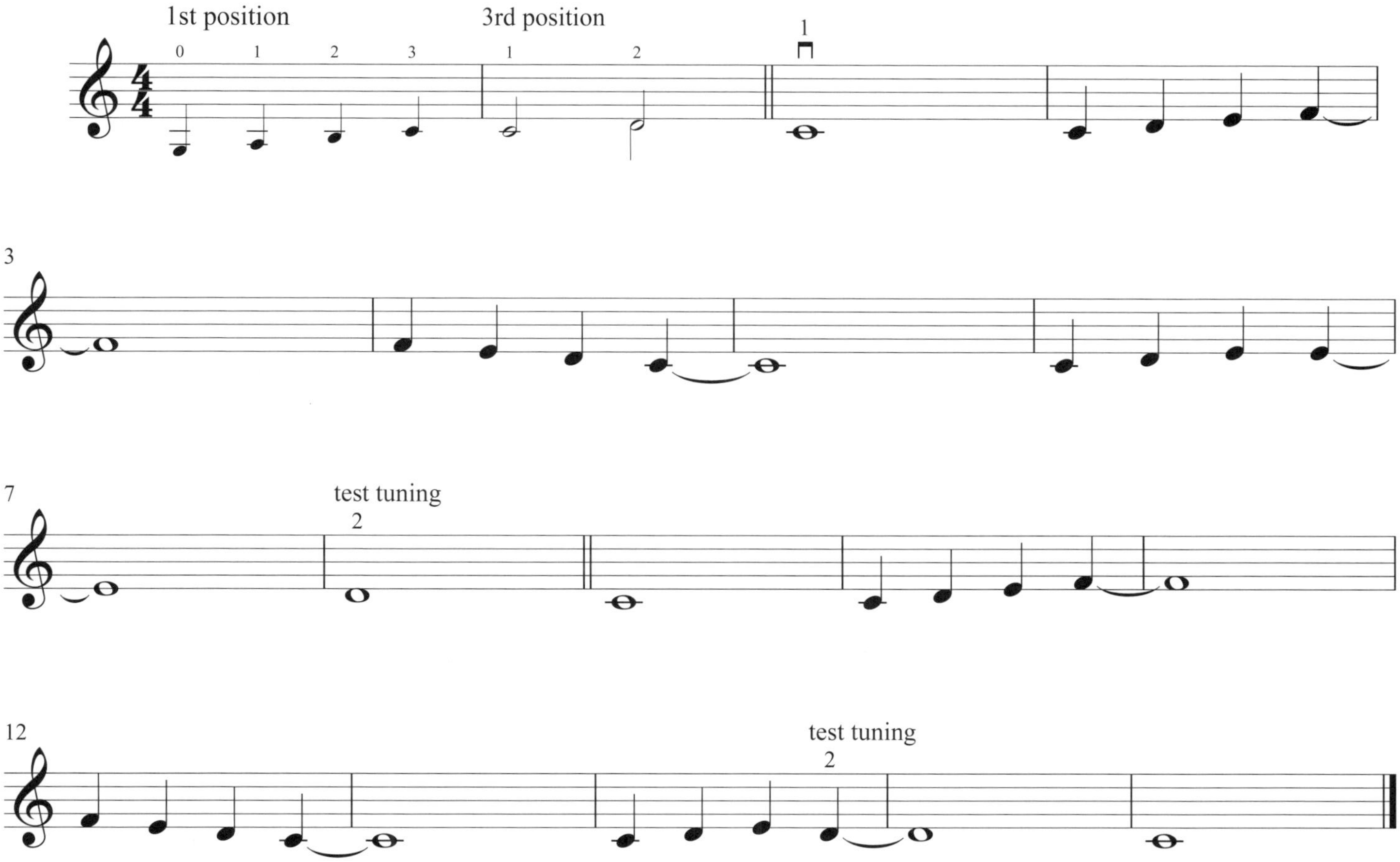

VIOLIN TALK

Testing the tuning of your fingers time and again will help you develop a feeling for the geography of the fingerboard.

Pieces in the First and Third Positions

In the previous exercises, we practiced the notes in the third position on the different strings. In real pieces, some sections of the music are played in the first position and other sections in the third position. The fingering in the music will indicate which position you will be playing in. While you will be able to decide on your own fingering later on, at this stage, it is wise to follow all the fingerings that are printed in your music. Play slowly until you get used to the position changes.

In "Habanera," you will change to the third position in bar 28. At bar 32, go back to first position, and at bar 34, back to third position until the end of the piece. Fingerings above the notes indicate what position you are playing in.

Take a look at the key signatures. You start with one flat and change to two sharps in bar 19.

Watch the accompanying video for a demonstration. You can ignore the three bars of rest at the start; the violin part begins in bar 4.

TOOLBOX

Sixteenth Note Triplets

Sixteenth note triplets fit into the time of one eighth note (half a beat).

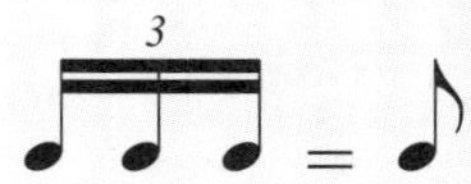

HABANERA

from CARMEN

By Georges Bizet

In "O Mio Babbino Caro," we can use the third position to make our piece more musically convincing. When playing slurs, aim to avoid unnecessary string crossings, as these might undo some of the smoothness we are trying to establish. A good example is bar 3. When we play this bar in the third position, we play the first three notes on the same string and avoid skipping a string when going from the low G to high G.

Another reason why we may use the third position is to give the same notes a different timbre. Observe this with the Gs in bars 17 and 18. The first G is quieter, which we achieve by playing the G in the third position on the A-string. The G in bar 18 will then sound more fresh and direct when we play it in the first position on the E-string.

Watch the video for more tips on bowing and shifting between positions.

O MIO BABBINO CARO

from GIANNI SCHICCHI

By Giacomo Puccini

VIOLIN TALK

Always change positions slowly. You will increase your accuracy and clarity in sound.

LESSON 18:
Trills and Grace Notes

Trills are the rapid alteration of two notes. They are played with the finger that is one note above the printed note in the music. Trills follow the key signature of the piece. In the next exercise, the trill is played F♯-G♯, a whole step between your fingers. Be aware that when you play a trill, the fingers tend to get closer together, so listen very carefully to the tuning.

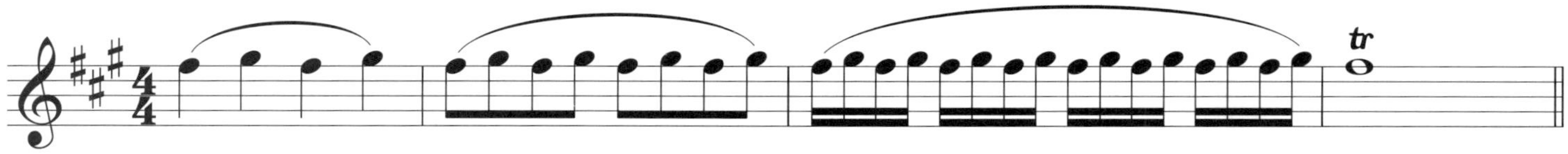

Practicing Spring

- Start with a martelé bow stroke at the upper half of the bow. On the dotted quarter note, try to get to the middle of the bow, but no further.
- We have four sharps in the key signature, which means that there is an F♯, C♯, G♯, and D♯. There is a raised third finger on the A-string, but on the E-string, the third finger is normal.
- When you get to the high C♯ in bar 8, stretch your fourth finger, and play the B with the third finger. Move down again while you play the open E. In bar 9, do the same thing, but stay up until you come down 3-3 in bar 10.
- When playing the trills, pick up your fingers as high as you can.
- For a real challenge, end this piece in the third position on the final note.

SPRING

from THE FOUR SEASONS

A *grace note* or crushed note is a note that is played very fast and sounds almost as if you made a mistake, which you rectified swiftly. Grace notes are represented as smaller notes in the music. There are various types of grace notes, but we will be learning the grace note as it is printed in Boccherini's "Minuet," with a slash through the note. Its official name is *acciaccatura*. Note that the trill in bar 7 also has a grace note before it. Even if the grace note had not been printed, you would still have played the trill in the same way; as in Baroque music, trills will mostly start on the upper note.

Practicing Minuet

"Minuet" is a piece with several repeats, and while some of these are straightforward, let's have a look at the three repeats in bars 21-23.

- Bar 21 goes back to bar 10.
- On the second time, skip bar 21 and play bar 22, the "second ending."
- At bar 22, skip bar 23 and play bar 24, "Moderato." We will save bar 23 for the end of the piece (*Fine*, means "the end" in Italian).
- At bar 48, notice the *D.C. al Fine*. Play *Da Capo*—from the head—the top of the piece to *Fine* in bar 23. When playing Da Capo, we do not play any repeats, so after bar 20, jump to bar 23, the Fine bar.

Other things of note:

- When playing the grace note at the start of the piece, have your second, third, and fourth fingers ready to play. As soon as you start to bow, take your fourth finger away. Do the same thing in bar 2.
- Bar 8, slur the sixteenth notes into the first note of the repeat.
- Bars 5 and 6, use martelé up bows.
- Bar 24, play spiccato, and remember to play at the balance point of the bow.
- Bars 25 and 27, lift your bow off the string on the staccato eighth notes.
- Bar 30, play legato, and switch back to spiccato in bar 31.
- Bar 33 (and similar bars), lower your right elbow, and have your third finger already on the string to make an easy transition to the E-string.

MINUET

from THE STRING QUINTET IN E MAJOR, OP. 11, NO. 5

By Luigi Boccherini

Milestone 5

You can play longer and more challenging pieces in the first and third positions with trills and grace notes. You have made outstanding progress.

LESSON 19:
Vibrato

Vibrato is a gentle raising and lowering of the pitch of a note to create a musical or creative effect. On the violin, there are different types of vibrato: arm, hand, and finger vibrato, which can be used depending on the style of the music played.

In general, less vibrato is used in Baroque music than in Romantic or modern music, although there are different "schools" of thought regarding vibrato playing. At the end of the Baroque period, Leopold Mozart, one of the leading violin pedagogues at the time, observed, "There are performers who tremble consistently on each note as if they had the permanent fever," suggesting that vibrato should be used only on sustained notes and at the ends of phrases when used as an ornament. However, in modern performances of classical music in concert halls and on television, vibrato is consistently used to enhance tone quality and to produce a big sound, which can fill large concert venues.

In this chapter, you will learn how to play using arm vibrato. You are ready to start learning to play with vibrato once you have reached a sufficiently relaxed mode of playing with your left hand. Being able to play with greater relaxation appears at different times for different players. This is a natural process and there is little you can do to spur this development. Therefore, if you find that your vibrato is not emerging yet right now, it is okay to leave it for a while and have another go in three to six months.

Preliminary Exercises

1. Slide each finger up and down the A-string. Always use the same part of your finger to slide. After doing this exercise you should have a single track on your fingertip.
2. Slide your finger at a consistent pace. Count a steady beat or use a metronome to help accomplish this.
3. Using the finger that feels the most comfortable, slide your finger back and forth and then pick a spot on the string to stop your finger as if a drop of super glue was put on your finger. Your elbow should keep moving as before. Keep your knuckles very soft. They should bend and stretch as you move your elbow.
4. Practice starting the vibrato movement without sliding first. Try on all four fingers.
5. Add the bow. Pick any spot on the fingerboard, start with your most comfortable finger and move slowly.
6. Move your finger at a steady pace and slowly increase speed.

Start by playing vibrato only on the longest notes in your music. Hold the long notes even longer until the vibrato gets going. Once you feel comfortable, you can add vibrato on shorter notes too.

"Sailing" is a lovely slow tune for you to practice vibrato. Take your time to allow the vibrato to emerge on the long notes. This might take a few seconds on each new note and is acceptable when you first start to play with vibrato. If your fingers slip a bit, that's okay at this stage. For now, focus on getting the vibrato going. Later, you will find that you can play vibrato without slipping.

SAILING

Words and Music by Gavin Sutherland

Practicing We Are the Champions

In "We Are the Champions," there are lots of long notes for you to practice your vibrato. In bars 25-26 and 81-85, there are suggestions for you to play in the third position to enable you to play notes with vibrato that in the first position would not be possible.

Practice playing this song in two ways:

1. Hold all notes for much longer than written. This helps establish a good sound and build endurance for sustaining your vibrato.
2. Slap your finger on the string and use the momentum created by the movement to start your vibrato instantly. This works well when the note you are using vibrato on is different than the note before, like in bars 16-17.

WE ARE THE CHAMPIONS

Demo/Backing

Words and Music by Freddie Mercury

Practicing The Entertainer

- Practice "slapped on" vibrato (see "We Are the Champions").
- Play at the upper or middle part of the bow. It is difficult to play fast notes at the lower part of the bow. You can steer yourself away from the lower half by stressing the first beat of the bar.

Watch the video for a detailed explanation of bow distribution in this song.

THE ENTERTAINER

By Scott Joplin

VIOLIN TALK

Match the speed of your vibrato to the style of your piece. Play slow pieces with a slower and wider vibrato, and faster pieces with a shorter and faster vibrato.

LESSON 20:
Harmonics

While the string normally vibrates along its entire length, when we play *harmonics*, we touch the string very lightly with our finger, and the string vibrates on either side of the finger. This produces a flute-like sound, called a harmonic or flageolet. The overtones are whistling sounds that create a lovely, bright effect in music. There are two types of harmonics: *natural harmonics* which we will learn to play here, and *artificial harmonics* where you stop the string with one finger and then play the harmonic with a different finger.

When we touch the string very lightly—without pressing down completely—at exactly the middle of the string, the string will sound an octave higher. This is indicated in the music with a little ° above the note. You can find this harmonic on each of the strings when you touch the string about 2cm past the rim of the violin. The trick with playing harmonics is to have a very light finger, but a strong bow stroke.

In notated music, the note is written at the pitch that the string will sound. For example, to play a harmonic on the G-string, the note will be written on the second line of the staff (normally played on the D-string), but we are actually bowing on the G-string.

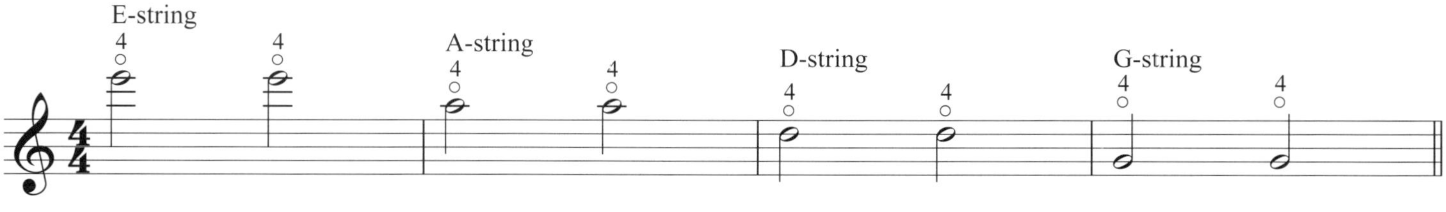

In bar 17 of "Chason de Matin," the harmonic is used to create a contrast between the two Ds. The harmonic is softer in quality, while the D played with the third finger sounds more direct. *Dolce* in the music means "sweetly."

CHANSON DE MATIN

By Edward Elgar

SOLVEIG'S SONG

from PEER GYNT

By Edvard Grieg

LESSON 21:
Chords

In addition to being able to play double stops (two notes together), we can also play combinations of 3 and 4 notes to create *chords*. Even though the music shows notes stacked on top of one another, we play the notes two-by-two. In 3-note chords, we play the lower two notes, followed by the middle and top note (doubling the middle note). In 4-note chords, we play the lower two notes, followed by the top two notes. Make a habit of always reading chords from the lowest note up.

When playing chords, we execute the string crossings with the right elbow. Practice slowly until you can find the correct strings with your bow without looking. Make sure your bow is parallel to the bridge and have your fingers ready on the needed pitches.

Listen to the ringing sound of the lower notes. These are the basis of your chords. The top notes of the chords are often part of a melody. While the lower half of the chord is the warm base, let the top part come out brightly if you can. Remember that the bass notes will still maintain their sound while you play the top notes.

Watch the video for more strategies on playing chords.

Practicing 3-Note Chords

Practicing 4-Note Chords

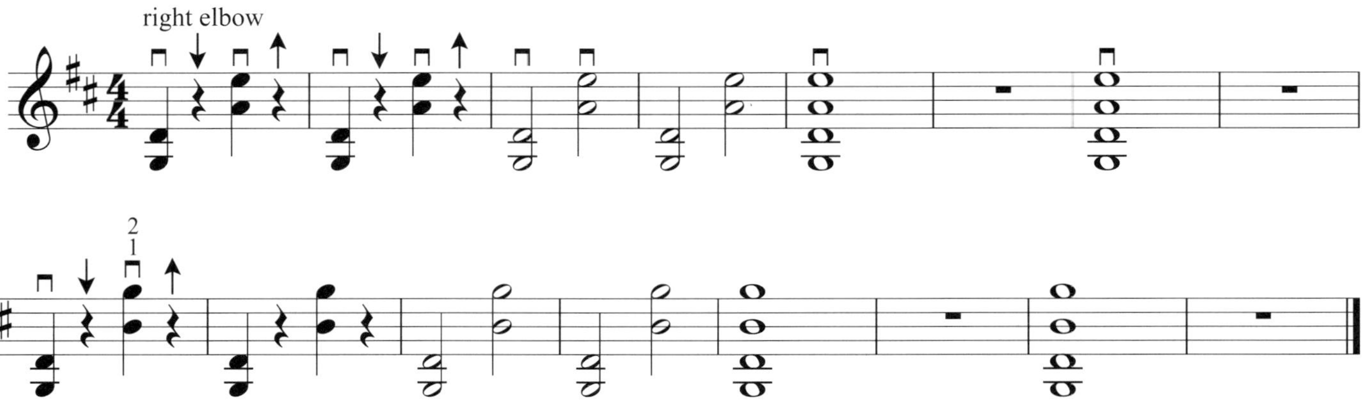

VIOLIN TALK

Take your time to make a beautiful string crossing when playing chords rather than rushing the chord.

In "Happy Birthday to You," use the long note at the fermatas to practice your vibrato.

HAPPY BIRTHDAY TO YOU

Words and Music by Mildred J. Hill and Patty S. Hill

MILESTONE 6

You can play violin pieces in different keys, in two positions with expression, and special techniques like harmonics and chords. That is simply magnificent. Well done!

LESSON 22:
Putting Everything Together

This chapter contains complete songs, in which you put everything together that you have learned in this book. All the techniques that you have learned are represented in these pieces. The pieces are an example of how the techniques are used not just in practice, but in real violin playing.

Practicing Chasing Cars

When you play "Chasing Cars," the notes are quite manageable. It's the repeats that may be a bit more challenging initially.

Once you understand the form of the music, play along with the original recording.

> **TOOLBOX**
>
> **D.S. al Coda**
>
> D.S. stands for *Del Segno* (the sign). When you see D.S., jump backward in the music to where you see this symbol 𝄋. *Coda* means "tail." After going back to the sign, when you reach "To Coda," jump to where you see a ⊕ and play to the end.

CHASING CARS

Words and Music by Gary Lightbody, Tom Simpson, Paul Wilson, Jonathan Quinn and Nathan Connolly

29
33
To Coda
2
p
38
2
44
48
D.S. al Coda
CODA
56
60
64
68
p
73
2

Practicing Gymnopédie No. 1

"Gymnopédie No. 1" is originally a piece for piano. Listen to the original if you have never heard it before. "Gymnopédie No. 1" is another example of how you can use the third position as a means of expression. For example, in bars 26-27, stay on the A-string to get a softer sound, compared to if you played the same notes on the E-string.

When playing long notes, drop your shoulder and right arm, stretch the bow arm forward, and move the bow slowly. Whenever the main theme comes in, slide into the first note rather than fixing the bow on the string. So, hold the bow high above the string, sliding down as it contacts the string. This gives you a nice starting note that eases into the string.

Composers often write expression markings in their native language. Satie writes in French "Lent et douloureux," which means "slow and painfully." Finding out what these terms mean before you play will help you express more easily what this piece is about.

GYMNOPÉDIE NO. 1 Demo/Backing

By Erik Satie

4
p
p
p

You will have noticed that there are several quick position changes in "Let It Go." Practice the shifts very slowly until you can find the destination note with your eyes closed. Your changes should be as smooth as possible in the left hand without being noticeable in the bowing technique.

LET IT GO

Demo/Backing

from FROZEN

Music and Lyrics by Kristen Anderson-Lopez and Robert Lopez

MILESTONE 7

You can work out new pieces independently. You have made fantastic progress. Congratulations on finishing this book and best wishes for your future violin playing.

APPENDIX

Answers to the most frequently asked questions. Further support is available from the Pro-Am Strings YouTube channel: ***www.youtube.com/c/ProAmStrings***.

The Bow

I cannot reach the point of the bow when I am playing long bows.
This is a very common issue and one that is relatively easy to cure. When you cannot reach the point of the bow, the most likely cause is that your bow arm is too far to your side, rather than in front. Check that your right upper arm is moving forward rather than staying by the side of your body. Try to stretch your bow arm further forward when you play a down bow. Your bow arm should be so far forward that at the end of your bow stroke, your hand is straight in front of you and your bow is parallel to the bridge.

My bow is slipping across the strings.
First, do you have enough rosin on your bow? Second, is your bow moving parallel to the bridge? See the question above. Third, is the level of your right elbow suitable for the string you are playing on?

My bow makes a scratchy sound while playing.
This may be caused by having either too much or too little rosin on your bow. If you find a thick layer of rosin dust on your violin after playing, wipe this off with a soft cloth and stop applying rosin for a few days. If there is not a speck of dust and the bow sometimes makes no sound at all or makes an intermittent sound, try applying more rosin. Another cause for your scratchy sound may be because you are holding the bow too tightly. Try softening your bow hand and see if this improves the sound you make.

The Left Hand

I cannot reach the strings with the third and fourth fingers of my left hand.
If you are unable to reach the strings with the third or fourth fingers of your left hand, the most likely reason is that your left elbow is not far enough under the violin. Bring your left elbow further in front of your belly. When your left elbow pivots to the right, your fingers swing more to the left above the fingerboard, provided that your left wrist is straight. Moving your wrist further out should also pivot your fingers further towards the strings. While you are checking the position of your left arm and hand, also check that your fingers are up above the fingerboard from the joint at the base of your fingers.

How much pressure should I apply to my fingers?
You should apply only as much pressure as is necessary to press the string against the fingerboard. Any more pressure will not add anything to your playing and is just a wasted effort. It will increase tension in your hand and will slow your playing down. Try instead to lighten your fingers if you can.

My left thumb is stiff and sore.
This happens to many new players. Whenever we try to learn a new skill, we use far too much energy to achieve our goals. Over time you will be able to relax more and your left thumb should become less sore. You may also try to relax your thumb during playing. For instance, wriggle your thumb whenever you have an open string or a rest in your music.

The Right Hand

Should my right-hand fingers always be relaxed?

Yes and no! Your bow hand should be relaxed so that you can make a beautiful sound. If you hold the bow too tightly, your tone might be scratchy. Your default bow hold, therefore, should be soft and relaxed. However, as we have practiced in this book, when you play staccato, and in particular martelé bowing, you will need to deliberately squeeze your bow hand to create the staccato sound.

My right-hand little finger is too short.

If your little finger cannot reach the bow, it is likely that your bow hand is pronating too much. This means that you are turning your right wrist to the left—as if you are pouring a cup of tea—and you are leaning towards your index finger too much. Try to balance your hand more evenly so that the ridge of your knuckles becomes more horizontal. In other words, try to twist your wrist to the right.